RIVER

RIVER

A Hudson Memoir

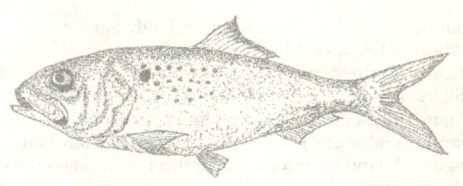

LESLIE DAY

Foreword by Ed Bacon

☰ **THREE** HILLS

AN IMPRINT OF CORNELL UNIVERSITY PRESS

ITHACA AND LONDON

First published 2025 by Cornell University Press

Printed in the United States of America

Title page figure: Atlantic menhaden. Illustration by Trudy Smoke.
Page v figure: Illustration of Leslie Day by Jessica Maffia.
Chapter 1 opening figure: Northern pipefish. Illustration by Trudy Smoke.
Chapter 2 opening figure: Moon jelly. Illustration by Trudy Smoke.
Chapter 3 opening figure: Blue crab. Illustration by Trudy Smoke.
Chapter 4 opening figure: Lion's mane jellyfish. Illustration by Trudy Smoke.
Chapter 5 opening figure: Atlantic sturgeon. Illustration by Trudy Smoke.
Chapter 6 opening figure: American eel. Illustration by Trudy Smoke.
Epilogue opening figure: Striped bass. Illustration by Jonah Nishiura.

Librarians: A CIP catalog record for this book is available from the Library of Congress.

ISBN 9781501783883 (paperback)
ISBN 9781501783869 (pdf)
ISBN 9781501783876 (epub)

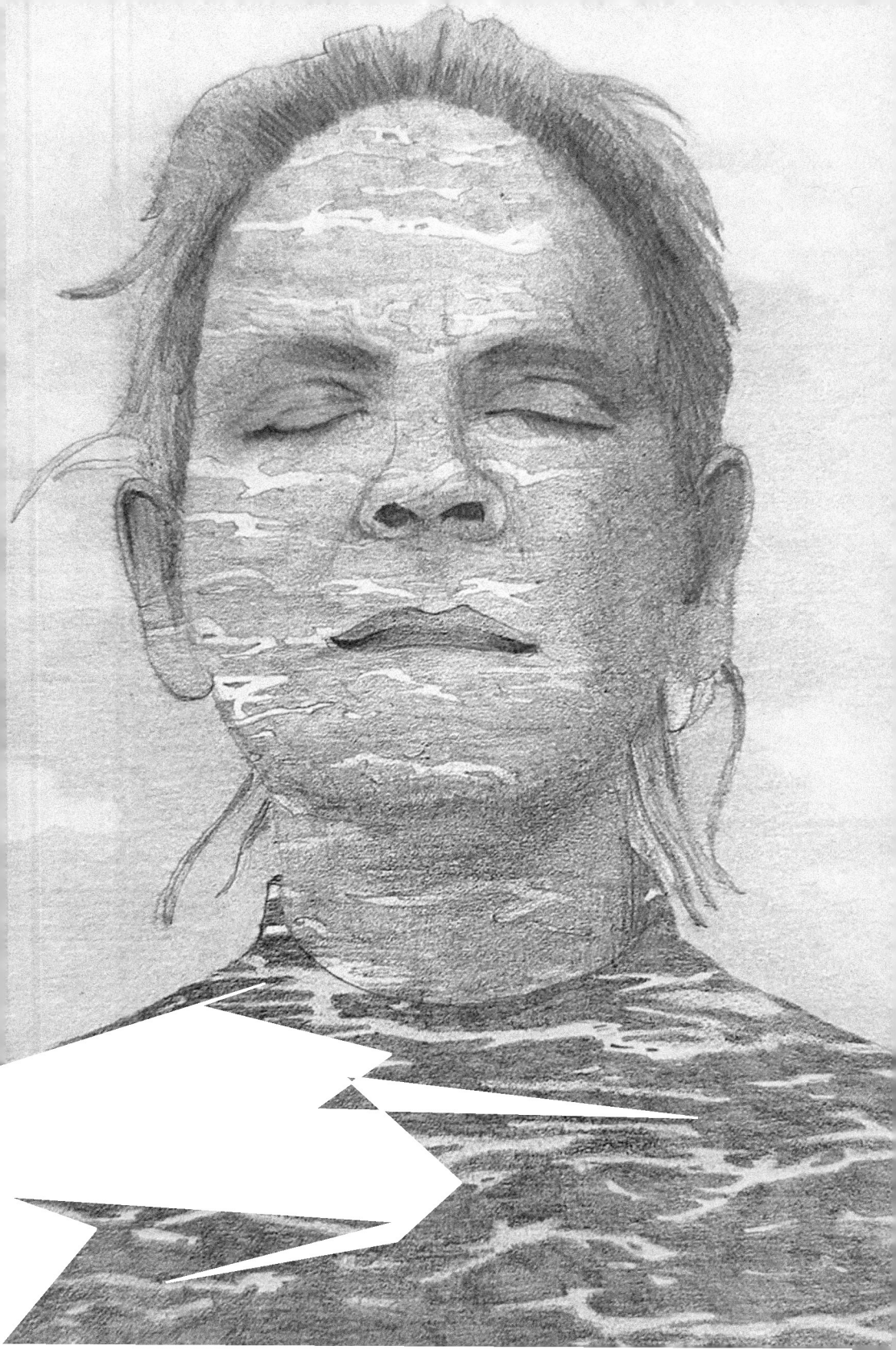

River is dedicated to

Faith Avedon Wohl, my dear stepmother,
who pushed me to write this book,

my friends and neighbors of the 79th Street
Boat Basin diaspora, who helped create our floating
pueblo magico, our magical village,

and to my darling granddaughter, Aya,
whose generation will one day be stewards of
the great Hudson River.

CONTENTS

Foreword by Ed Bacon   ix

Preface   xi

1. What the Water Holds   1

2. Homecoming: The 79th Street Boat Basin   13

3. Student, Teacher: River Lessons   43

4. River Life: Inhabitants of the Hudson   61

5. Weathering: Storms and Other Threats to the
   79th Street Boat Basin   95

6. Goodbyes   119

Epilogue: River Resources   127

Acknowledgments   137

Notes   141

Bibliography   149

Index   157

CONTENTS

FOREWORD

In 1970, I traded my suburban life for a houseboat at the 79th Street Boat Basin on Manhattan's Upper West Side. As soon as I stepped into that magical village, I knew I'd found my true home.

In 1975, a flower child named Leslie Day traded her city apartment for a houseboat, also changing her life forever.

The Basin was a diverse community—celebrities, Broadway dancers, singers, artists, and authors mingled with CEOs, corporate workers, entrepreneurs, and the unemployed. At one time, seventeen nationalities were represented, not to mention the full spectrum of home life: single, living together, married, kids, divorced, gay, lesbian, and asexual. The common thread among all was a love of boats and of the water.

Living on a boat was like being in a womb with a view. The ceaseless urban street noise was replaced by the gentle lapping of waves, and the community provided a warm and nurturing social milieu.

As we read about Day's intertwined relationships with the Basin's boaters, the community, and the river in these pages, we are invited to join her journey of learning and discovery. The Basin was her laboratory, her family home, and her inspiration for teaching.

Day connects her scientific forays to her life's events with a disarming sense of wonder. We learn about the challenges of living aboard—the river ice floes, the storms, the city's opposition and neglect, all of which have threatened the Basin's existence. Even to this day, the fight continues to keep the magical village open for the future.

I hope that readers will come away from this book with a fresh understanding of what it means to find one's place in the world, to find *home*— which is not just the place but also its people. As you read *River*, you'll understand how our flower child blossomed into a Renaissance woman at the Boat Basin, earning her doctorate, her New Jersey Teacher of the Year award, and praise for her other books on New York City's nature, trees, birds, and even the honeybees of the Waldorf Astoria.

Ed Bacon

79th Street Boat Basin liveaboard for fifty-two years

PREFACE

The need to be near water drew me to living on boats. Unless you are in the water, there is nothing as close to it as being on a boat. A houseboat with a place to lay my head, cook my food, read my books, and be with my loved ones was the answer to my dreams. Now at the age of eighty, I have lived almost my entire adult life in houseboats at the 79th Street Boat Basin on the Hudson River in Manhattan. New York, New York, as the song goes. So nice they named in twice.

My love of water and of the life within and around it is like a magnet, pulling me into a passion for nature and my life's calling as a student and teacher of the natural sciences. I have a deep love for the river and its animals, zooplankton, and phytoplankton that make it a thriving ecosystem and a place of great beauty.

I have already written four books about the natural world of New York City, but this one ties together my life, my work, my love, and my passion for my city and its river. The Hudson carries the story of Manhattan and its millions of lives with it as it flows north and south past the island.

I dedicate this book to the past, current, and future generations who have cared for, do care for, and will care for the Hudson. To those who, like me, are drawn to its beauty, its history, its important ecological role, and who share a love and concern for its wildlife.

I also dedicate this book to those who have not yet opened their eyes and hearts to this river, in the hopes that this book will help them see the river and fall in love.

Leslie Day

August 2025
Riverdale, New York

RIVER

Chapter 1

WHAT THE WATER HOLDS

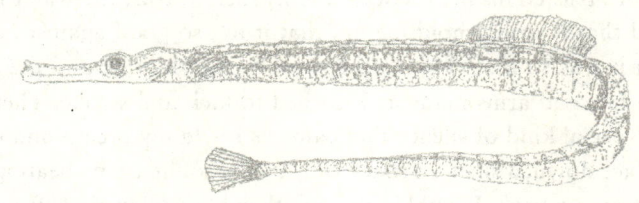

Dawn emerges from the night, and the morning light drifts toward me across the Hudson. The colors of the sky change from twilight blue, to yellow, to orange, to pink, and then pale blue, blending into one another like watercolors. As the sun continues to rise, the river sparkles like diamonds, and my four-year-old mind thinks that the water must be covered in jewels.

That was the view from my childhood bedroom in Englewood Cliffs, New Jersey, in a tiny cottage rented to us by the owner of a large estate. The house itself sat atop the Palisades, a rock wall that stretches forty miles from Jersey City, New Jersey, to Haverstraw, New York. From Jersey City, the wall gradually rises, and by the time it reaches Weehawken some five miles away it is two hundred feet tall. Weehawken (Wee-haw-ken) is a Lenape word that means "rocks that look like trees."

More than seventy-six years have passed since my time at the cottage, but I can still see it all so clearly. Though we moved several times in my youth, our home on the Palisades holds some of my most formative memories. And it was there, too, that I first fell in love with the Hudson and the magic of water.

After we moved to the cottage, I remember my father announcing, "It's time for you to learn to swim."

I wasn't afraid—anything I did with my dad was fun. He was my great protector in all things, and I always felt safe as long as he was there. On Saturday mornings we drove over the George Washington Bridge into Manhattan to a pool in the basement of the Henry Hudson Hotel on West 57th Street. I remember him walking along the side of the pool, his loud voice barking out instructions, teaching me first how to do the dead man's float, then the crawl, and then how to breathe between strokes.

Thinking that the best way to teach me was from the side of the pool, my father never once put a toe in the water while showing me how to swim. But I trusted his instructions and learned to trust the water in turn. I learned that it would hold me up, that it felt so good against my skin, and that it was so blue. I loved the smell of the chlorine and the sounds my little feet and arms made as I learned to kick and stroke. Then there was the special kind of silence that came as I held my breath and learned to float face down, a silence broken only by the sound of my beating heart.

While on my back, I could look up with eyes wide open, drifting to the rhythm of my breath rising and falling and to the sound of my father's voice: "That's right, Les. Good job. You're doing great."

I felt loved, supported by his voice and by the water.

My father was originally a Jersey boy. At the turn of the twentieth century, his parents, Jacob and Sadie Wohl, immigrated from Europe to New York City when they were in their teens—he from Vienna, Austria, and she from a small town in Romania. They met, fell in love, and married on the Lower East Side of Manhattan, eventually settling in Union City in Hudson County, New Jersey, where they opened a necktie factory. My grandmother, a smart, hardworking businesswoman, ran the shop where six women sat at sewing machines, making the ties from beautiful colored silk. I remember going there with my father and collecting silky swatches in every color of the rainbow. Every day at lunch, my grandmother would cook a meal for her employees, and they'd all sit down together at a long wooden table and eat her brisket and *kasha varnishkes*, among other heavy kosher meals. My grandfather ran the little tie shop in the tie factory's storefront on Bergenline Avenue, in Union City. My grandparents told me how beautiful New Jersey's little towns were then—the tree-lined streets, lovely homes, and gardens of Weehawken and Union City. My

Figure 1. Leslie and her father, 1946.

father, Howard, was born in Union City in 1919 and grew up in those river towns. But what *he* recalled was the strong draw of Manhattan and how much he loved to ride the ferry into the city when he was still just a boy.

It was the early 1930s—the age of boats carrying people from New Jersey, Staten Island, Brooklyn, Queens, and the Bronx back and forth across the Hudson and East Rivers to Manhattan Island. The ferry was cheap and romantic, and my father, a skinny and pugnacious adolescent, watched the skyline and listened to the hum of the city as it all moved closer and closer to him. Crossing the Hudson meant freedom and a life away from parents who were grieving the loss of his twenty-one-year-old sister, Lillian, to leukemia. It was a river of dreams, carrying him toward independence, money, and the possibility of an exciting life. He regularly skipped school to make money selling newspapers in Times Square or playing craps in the streets of Manhattan.

Unable to rein him in, my grandparents eventually sent my father to a military school in Georgia. He was in high school there when his cousin introduced him to my mother, Adele Wachtel, during a summer visit home. My mother attended a high school in Woodmere, Long Island, but the two sent letters back and forth during the following school year.

In 1938, after my mother graduated high school, her parents, Lena and Julian Wachtel, moved to West 73rd Street in Manhattan. My father would visit her and play baseball in the ball field along the Hudson River near the 79th Street Boat Basin, and my mom would walk down to the river to watch him play. My parents married in 1940. I was born in August 1945 at the end of World War II, and my brother, David, was born three years after.

When I was thirty, I told my father that I was moving to a boat at the 79th Street Boat Basin. Though many years had passed by then, he easily recalled the joy of those sun-filled days—playing ball, watching the river and the boats, and seeing my teenage mother walking toward him, her beautiful red hair gleaming in the sunlight.

My father was a gifted storyteller. He was the most entertaining human I knew as a child. I was fascinated and charmed by his love of life, music, dancing, singing, and being silly and fun to spend time with.

One of the most dramatic early childhood memories I have of my father is tied to the George Washington Bridge. From my bedroom window in that cottage on the Palisades, I could see the bridge. It had been built in 1931, fourteen years before I was born. Though the city had been exploring the idea of a bridge connecting Manhattan and New Jersey since the 1880s, it wasn't until bridge engineer Othmar Ammann proposed the current site that it seemed feasible and became a reality.[1] The bridge was constructed exactly where it could be anchored into the Palisades on the Jersey side and the exposed Manhattan schist on the New York side. Close to a mile long and, at the time of this writing, almost a hundred years old, it continues to serve the millions of people who travel back and forth from New Jersey to Manhattan and beyond each year.

As a little child I hated to be separated from my father, even for a day. I had a rising sense of dread as he left for work each morning, his car winding down the long driveway toward the gates of the estate. I could see the George Washington Bridge from our house, and I knew that bridge was the route my father took to work in Manhattan.

One day I came up with a scheme to stay with him, and I planned it with great care. Early in the morning, as he was getting ready, I dressed and snuck into the back of the car where I hid on the floor. This was 1949. I was only four years old, but I still recall everything about that morning.

My father got into the car as usual and drove the mile or so to the bridge. My idea had been to surprise him when he parked the car at work in Manhattan, but halfway over the bridge I couldn't control myself. I jumped up from my hiding place and yelled, "Hi, Daddy!"

Instead of the happy reception I'd expected, he reached around and grabbed the back of my shirt, screaming, "Your mother will think you fell off the cliff!"

Of course, there were no cell phones back then, so he had to come off the bridge, turn around at West 178th Street on the Manhattan side, and take me back home, all the while yelling how he'd be late for work. He was furious, and I was devastated.

Here I was thinking he'd be so happy that we could spend the day together instead of apart. But the bridge that I thought would carry me to a day of happiness ended up being a bridge to my first experience of humiliation and shame. Before that day he had never been mad at me. He had never even raised his voice. I truly thought he had stopped loving me.

We left our little cottage on the Palisades a year after we moved in. The Palisades Interstate Park Commission was close to building the new Palisades Interstate Parkway, and the estate our home was part of would be torn down during construction of the parkway. In hindsight, I realized that was why the owner of the estate moved away and rented out the cottage in the first place. He knew his estate and all others between the George Washington Bridge and the Bear Mountain Bridge would be torn down not only to make way for the parkway but also to leave the Palisades in their natural state without homes or buildings of any kind.

The Palisades were formed more than two hundred million years ago when an intrusion of volcanic magma was injected between layers of sandstone as the supercontinent Pangaea was breaking apart. Eventually, the magma solidified into an incredibly hard rock called diabase. Over millions of years, the sandstone eroded, leaving the diabase exposed, a powerful remnant of a geological upheaval that changed the face of the earth a quarter of a billion years ago.[2]

However, in the mid-nineteenth century, the need for the diabase to build New York City's streets, piers, and skyscraper foundations was

Figure 2. Carpenter Brothers' Quarry blasting the Palisades below Fort Lee, New Jersey, 1900. Courtesy of the Palisades Interstate Park Commission.

leading to the destruction of the cliffs. Quarrymen began blasting the ancient wall with dynamite. Manhattan residents could hear the explosions and see the ochre scars and rubble. This was at a time when the painters of the Hudson River School were portraying the river and the Palisades as icons of untamed nature. Many were outraged at the destruction of the scenic beauty across from the bustling and rapidly growing city.[3]

The first people to spring into action to fight the quarrying were a group of New Jersey women. They created the Englewood chapter of the New Jersey State Federation of Women's Clubs with the express purpose of stopping the demolition of the Palisades.[4] The Englewood chapter joined forces with the American Scenic and Historic Preservation Society, New York City's first association of its kind. The society was created and led by Andrew Haswell Green, who was dubbed the "Father of New York City" for his many accomplishments. These two groups eventually received financial backing from John D. Rockefeller Sr. and J. P. Morgan. George Perkins was Morgan's business partner and a staunch conservationist, philanthropist, and owner of the Wave Hill estate in Riverdale. Perkins could hear the explosions from his home across the river from the Palisades. Not only was he outraged by the destruction, but the blasts kept waking up his sleeping toddler.[5]

The women of the Englewood chapter of the New Jersey Federation of Women's Clubs, who could not even vote at the time, lobbied New Jersey

Governor Foster McGowan Voorhees, at first without success. Finally, Rockefeller, Perkins, Morgan, and others brought Teddy Roosevelt, then governor of New York, into the battle. Roosevelt was an avid naturalist and preservationist. His family had leased Wave Hill for a couple of years when he was a boy, and he had spent time exploring the Palisades as a young man.[6] By 1900, both Governor Voorhees and Governor Roosevelt had signed bills protecting the Palisades.

The two states jointly formed the Palisades Interstate Park Commission. Perkins was made commissioner and helped raise money to buy the estates and land on top of the cliffs for a newly formed park. He also convinced Morgan to contribute $125,000 to buy out the Carpenter Brothers, owners of the largest quarry destroying the Palisades. In this way, Perkins played a significant role in the preservation of the Palisades and the creation of the Palisades Interstate Park.[7]

Another individual who had a huge impact was John D. Rockefeller Jr. In 1917, he bought land in Washington Heights to build Fort Tryon Park, which looked out over the river to the Palisades. By the 1930s, he became heavily involved in protecting the Palisades from real estate developers. By 1933, Fort Tryon Park was almost complete, and Rockefeller Jr. kept buying up land on top of the Palisades, stipulating that the Palisades Interstate Park Commission could use the land only if they built a scenic parkway from the newly built George Washington Bridge to the Bear Mountain Bridge and that all preexisting structures be removed.[8] Thanks to Rockefeller's vision, New Yorkers from Washington Heights and Inwood in Manhattan to those along the river from the Bronx up through Westchester County can now look out at the untouched Palisades.

For my family, however, Rockefeller's stipulations meant that the cottage and estate we lived on would be bulldozed and removed. We had to leave our tiny piece of heaven, much to the delight of my grandparents who worried that their precious grandchildren might fall off the cliffs. This was no idle fear. There was no fencing on the estate on which our little house sat, and it was a terribly dangerous place for children. Once, my baby brother David started crawling toward the cliff's edge. Our beloved rescue dog Duke—a large, skinny, half German shepherd and half Belgian shepherd named for Duke Snider, my father's favorite Brooklyn Dodger—grabbed David's diaper and pulled him back to safety. The incident became a heart-stopping piece of family history.

Years later I learned that the significance of the Palisades extended well beyond our natural and infrastructure history; it shaped our cultural lexicon as well. During a ferry ride around the island of Manhattan in 2003 with the late great Sidney Horenstein, at the time a geologist emeritus at the American Museum of Natural History, I learned about the etymology of the term "cliffhanger."

In the early 1900s, Fort Lee, a town on top of the Palisades in New Jersey, became the country's first film capital. This was thanks to its proximity to the towering Palisades and the ever-running ferries, which brought over actors and film crews from Manhattan.

Continued-next-week serials, including *The Perils of Pauline*, which starred actress Pearl White and was produced by William Randolph Hearst, were filmed on the cliffs and led to the coining of the term "cliffhanger." It carried the double meaning of both the literal danger of falling over a steep precipice (a scenario that ended many of the serials) and the sensation of not knowing what was coming next. This evocation of danger and mystery is forever connected to the thrill and awe of the Palisades' majesty.[9]

If you hike north below the cliffs along the shore from the Englewood Boat Basin, you will eventually come upon an old cemetery that belonged to the tiny village of Undercliff, one of several hamlets settled in the early 1800s by Dutch families that also included Englewood Dock, Fisherman's Village, Bloomer's Beach, and Pickletown. Pickletown was named in the 1830s, when a sloop laden with cucumbers sank. The cucumbers were gathered as they washed ashore and pickled.[10]

Boatmen, fishermen, and quarrymen built their homes and gardens along the shore of the river at the base of the Palisades. All that is left of their villages is a small cemetery in what then was the village of Undercliff. Some of these headstones are more than two hundred years old, and very few are still legible: Belinda Woolsey, wife of George Bloomer, d. Mch. 19, 1843, aged 24 yrs. 3 mos.; Susan Van Wagener, d. Jan 11, 1811, wife of Charles Van Wagener; and Julia (Smith) Bloomer, wife of Theophilus H. Bloomer, and daughter of Rev. John and Sarah Smith, d. Jan. 5, 1837, aged 21 yrs. 11mos. and 26 days.[11]

As you walk farther north along the shore, you'll come upon ruins of what had been a popular bathhouse in the 1920s and 1930s, Bloomer's Beach, named for the Bloomer family that once lived in the fishing village.

Figure 3. Bathers in the Hudson River at Bloomer's Beach beneath the Palisades, summer 1932. Courtesy of the Palisades Interstate Park Commission.

Bloomer's Beach opened in 1922—a large, beautiful stone facility with showers, changing rooms, and thousands of lockers to accommodate the hundreds of thousands of New Yorkers who took the Englewood ferry from Dyckman Street in northern Manhattan across the river to escape the terrible summer heat and bathe in the still relatively clean waters of the Hudson. In the summers of 1922 and 1923, nearly one million people traveled on ferries to Bloomer's Beach and other beaches in the cool shade of the Palisades.[12]

At the beginning of World War II, the bathing beaches were closed. The Dyckman Street ferry was put out of service because of gasoline rationing, and the river became more polluted. The war effort up and down the river produced enormous amounts of industrial waste, some of which was dumped into the Hudson. The city of Yonkers alone had more than seventy-five companies that switched from producing consumer goods to producing products for the war, including clothing, blankets, parts for warships, cable for submarine oil pipelines below the English Channel, parachutes, lubricants, and torpedoes.[13] The cliffs were protected, but it would be decades before the river itself was protected by law against polluters.

In 1965, the Department of the Interior and the National Park Service designated the Palisades Interstate Park as a National Historic Landmark. A New Jersey bill noted that the Palisades "represents an extraordinary effort on the part of New Jersey and New York to preserve the scenic beauty of the cliffs on the lower western side of the Hudson River."[14] In 1983, the Palisades were named a National Natural Landmark as they were "the best example of a thick diabase sill formation known in the United States. Columnar jointing, an olivine zone and thermal metamorphic effects are attributes found in rare combination. . . . The glaciated crest provides impressive evidence of the Pleistocene glacier." As the Ice Age glacier moved south, it scoured the crest and left striations in the top of the cliffs—a unique geology well deserving of the status of a historic and natural landmark.[15]

In 2013, the electronics corporation LG attempted to build its headquarters on top of the Palisades in Englewood Cliffs. LG wanted to build a 143-foot-tall building, which would have extended way above the tree line and marred the Palisades. The corporation quickly found itself in a fight with preservationists and community organizations, including the Rockefeller family, Scenic Hudson, the New Jersey State Federation of Women's Clubs, the Natural Resources Defense Council, the New Jersey Conservation Foundation, and the New York-New Jersey Trail Conference.

The main concern of these groups was that the structure would be out of line with a local ordinance that capped Palisades building heights at thirty-five feet, and a variance might establish a precedent for tall buildings on the ridge north of the George Washington Bridge, ruining scenic views. The battle occurred on several fronts—through protests, ads, and a lawsuit. Articles in all the city's newspapers, billboards on Manhattan's Henry Hudson Parkway, and TV and talk-radio shows protesting the height of the proposed building brought public awareness to this potential blight on top of the Palisades. Some people boycotted LG and stopped buying their products.

Finally, in 2015, the parties agreed to a compromise for the building: it would be sixty-nine feet tall, a height that matched the height of the tree canopy of the area. Rockefeller Jr.'s grandson, Laurance Rockefeller Jr., an environmental lawyer, said in an interview in *The New York Times* that it was the chairman of LG, Bon-Moo Koo, an avid birdwatcher, who stopped the project. Rockefeller received a signed copy of *A Field Guide to the Birds of Korea*, for which Koo had written the introduction, along with a note that read, "I assure you that I have great respect for your family's passion for nature conservation and cultural heritage."[16]

Today, the Englewood Cliffs LG headquarters on Sylvan Avenue is a very long, low, glass building. Looking over at the Palisades from our home in Riverdale, I can barely see part of the rooftop of the LG headquarters where the trees are low; the rest of the building is blocked by the treetops of the Palisades.

My family eventually moved to Queens and from there to Long Island. Our shared love of water ensured that we went to Jones Beach every weekend in the summer and on our weeklong family vacations. When I was nine, we moved to Boat Lane, Levittown, Long Island—a town we chose because every neighborhood had its own swimming pool. Azalea Pool was the one that I rode my bike to every summer day until high school, when I got my first job as a cashier at Woolworth's.

The summer we moved to Levittown, in 1954, my father noticed the teenage boys, with their slicked-back ducktail hair, doing impressive dives off the high board. Swan dives, back dives, somersaults, twists, and flips—you name it. He asked them to teach him. A combination of horror and giddiness swept through me as I watched him land belly flop after belly flop, bellowing all the way into the water, until, after many tries, he became a good diver.

In Levittown, which in hindsight my father ironically called "Love It Town," my parents' marriage started to unravel. By the time I turned twelve, my worst fear came true. My father left.

Living without him was a lonely existence. I only saw him every other weekend and every other Thursday for dinner. Once a happy child who loved school and enjoyed discovering new things in nature, I now felt adrift and disconnected from many of my interests. It was like being at sea, tossed and churned by the undertow of abandonment. In the midst of this, water was one of the few things that still made me feel like myself. Water was my sanctuary.

My father moved to a small apartment in Long Beach, Long Island, a few blocks from the ocean. It was winter: cold, windy, and bleak. When we walked into his apartment, he would look at his fish tank and say, "Hello, fish." He was lonely, and it broke my heart.

Over time, he became close with Faith Avedon, a woman he worked with at his college yearbook business. Faith was seventeen years younger than my father, but she was wise beyond her years and brilliant. With an IQ of more than 190, she had attended Hunter College Elementary School—a city school that only admits children in the top 1 percent of intellectual ability. Then she went to the High School of Performing Arts.

Faith was a Renaissance woman—artist, writer, and problem-solver extraordinaire. She eventually carved out a brilliant career at DuPont as a champion of women balancing family life in a corporate world. From there she was hired by the Clinton White House and continued to work as director of the General Services Administration's Office of Workplace Initiatives in Washington, DC.

I was fourteen when I told my father he should marry Faith. I remember the exact conversation in his car on the way to Long Beach. He laughed—part stunned, maybe, and part grateful that I cared so much about him. (Near the end of her life, Faith told me that when my father had recounted that conversation to her and laughed again, she had said, "What's so funny?")

To my great relief, they married within a year and had three children: my brothers Bill and Mike and finally a little sister, Jennifer Wohl. For more than sixty years, Faith was a pillar of my life and the person I credit with saving my father by bringing love back into his life. In 2021, Faith died. We were only nine years apart in age, yet she was a lifetime older than me. My siblings and I will remain eternally grateful for her love and her counsel.

The day my father died, November 21, 1993, I left my houseboat and walked along the docks and the Riverside Park promenade. I wanted to escape the pain, but everywhere I looked I saw him: the 79th Street Boat Basin, the Palisades, the George Washington Bridge, the river, the Jersey shoreline, Riverside Park, the ball field. More than thirty years later, I continue to connect to my father in all the physical and emotional landmarks linked by the river. More than anyone in my life, it was my father who helped me understand what water can hold. And this knowledge led me to a marina in the heart of New York City where I would find my husband, create my own family and community, be surrounded by nature, and discover my life's work.

Chapter 2

HOMECOMING

The 79th Street Boat Basin

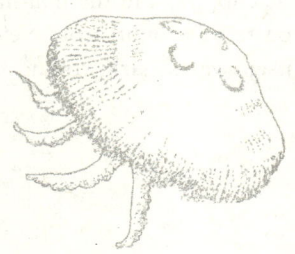

"Upper West Side, furnished, could call it a studio, river view, $150 a month." This was the ad I found in *The New York Times'* real estate section while sitting in a friend's car on West 72nd Street, waiting for alternate side of the street parking time to end. As soon as I got back to my apartment on West 73rd Street, I called the number in the ad and learned that this "studio" was in fact a houseboat, beautifully and perhaps serendipitously named *Mandala*. One of the meanings of the word "mandala" as defined by *The Oxford Dictionary of Phrase and Fable* is "a symbol in a dream, representing the dreamer's search for completeness and self-unity."[1] I was so excited by the prospect that I literally jumped up and down as I spoke to Sean, my potential new landlord.

Sean Disney, an architectural engineer who lived on City Island, had built this unusual little boat himself. He explained how he had created the ferro-cement hull in Staten Island—building a wooden frame with layers of chicken wire and metal rods and then covering the entire armature with cement. After the hull was complete, he built wooden cabins on top of it. Finally, he installed a small inboard engine in the hull and motored the vessel over to the 79th Street Boat Basin where he'd hoped to make it his home. Unfortunately for Sean, his fiancé did not share his enthusiasm for the little boat that he had crafted—thus, the real estate listing.

Afraid I might miss out on the unique opportunity to live on a houseboat in my Upper West Side neighborhood, I ran all the way down the hill from West 73rd Street to the 79th Street Boat Basin to have a look. It was an adorable boat and perfectly suited to my needs. All the furniture—couch, kitchen table, loft bed—was built right in. I gave Sean a check for fifty dollars as a hold, and I moved in just two weeks later, on Halloween night, 1975.

That first evening I stood on the dock in front of my boat. It was cold and windy. The river was choppy, and the floating dock I stood on was undulating like a rollercoaster. The lights from New Jersey twinkled in the distance, and the river itself was a dark, roiling shape. I thought, What have I done?

Adrift

The *Mandala* was not my first boat. In 1968, I moved from Manhattan to San Francisco with my then-husband Bill, an artist and a poet. He introduced me to the work of Anaïs Nin. I loved the language and characters in all of her books, but my favorite work of hers was *Collages*, a collection of short stories about women who lived on houseboats and barges around the world—on the Seine River in France, on the River Thames in Britain, and in Sausalito, California, on Richardson Bay, which is part of the San Francisco Bay ecosystem.

When Bill and I divorced in 1969, I saw an ad in the *San Francisco Chronicle* for a bedroom to rent in a floating home in Sausalito. I moved in with my cat Nessim and discovered the beauty of life on the water for the first time. The changing light and colors on the bay and in the sky, the gentle rocking of the boat, the camaraderie of the people who lived along the docks—I loved it all. I never knew life could be so colorful: peaceful yet dramatic, exciting yet calm. I had discovered my element.

After a few months, I found a boat that I could afford to rent by myself. The *William C* was a wooden ferryboat built in 1916 to carry schoolchildren back and forth across the Sacramento River. It was thirty-six feet long and only nine feet wide, with windows all around.

The only problem with the boat was that it was always taking on water. Pumps would go on in the middle of the night to pump out the bilge that was filling up. One morning I woke up in my narrow top bunk to see Nessim looking down intently. His head was moving back and forth, left to right, and back again. Water was covering the floor of the cabin, and he was watching my slippers float to and fro as the boat rocked from stem to stern.

I stayed on the *William C* until I moved to Vancouver Island, British Columbia, where life took yet another turn. I had been camping on Hornby Island in the Salish Sea, and I was walking through the island's old-growth forest one day when I thought I heard someone with a New York accent. I started running toward this voice, which turned out to belong to a young man about my age, with a beard and a woolen cap. Sure enough, he was from Brooklyn. Just hearing him speak, I was so flooded with homesickness that I started to cry. It was a tipping point. In 1971, after almost four years of living on the West Coast, I finally returned home.

Dawn came bright and clear on my first morning on the *Mandala*. The wind had died down, and sunlight sparkled on the water. Looking at the surface, I could see movement. Tides are vertical movements, deepening during incoming tides, and becoming shallow during outgoing tides. Currents are the horizontal movement of water, moving faster when the water is deeper and more slowly in shallows. Flood tide is when the water moves north from the Atlantic Ocean into the Hudson River. Ebb tide is when the water moves south from the river out to the ocean.

I would later learn more about how the tides outside my window were "patterns set by a celestial dance involving the earth, the moon, and to a lesser extent, the sun."[2] The gravitational pull by these large bodies in space causes the ocean water to swell and move into the Hudson River basin twice each day. Approximately six hours after each high tide, the ocean water recedes, causing low tide.

Living on the water full-time, I experienced not only two high and two low tides but also two slack tides in between high and low each day. Slack tide is when, for a short time, the river is perfectly still. High slack tide occurs when the incoming tide slows to a stop as it changes from flood to ebb. Low slack tide is when the ebb current briefly stops as it changes from ebb to flood. Slack tide can last fifteen to forty-five minutes. It is a reprieve, a stilling of the celestial forces of gravitational pull.

During a flood tide, as the swelling water flows into New York Harbor and north into the Hudson, the current runs fastest when there is a southerly wind. If there is a strong wind out of the north moving against the current, white caps appear as the wind and the tidal current face off against each other. This was when living on a boat could get uncomfortable. If it happened on a weekend, it was a good time to walk up to Broadway and go to a movie. If it happened during the night, you were not going to get much sleep—at least, not until the current slowed and the rocking stopped.

I did love the soft, constant movement of the boat. It created a physical peace within my body. This is why babies love to be rocked or why it's soothing to sit in a rocking chair or on a swing. The gentle back-and-forth movements are therapeutic and relaxing.

Acclimating to the rocking is called "getting your sea legs." It didn't take long for me to get mine, but after three weeks of living on the boat, I had a surprise on the platform of the number 1 downtown train. While I was waiting for it to pull into the station on West 79th and Broadway, the entire platform started to move: back and forth, up and down, and back and forth. I felt like I was hallucinating, but in fact I was getting my "land legs." There is a medical diagnosis for this—*mal de débarquement* syndrome—or "sickness of disembarkation." You feel like you're rocking even though you're not.

It never happened again, and after that I could easily transition from water to land and back to water without any odd experiences. My thirty-year-old brain had adjusted. Writing this at eighty, it has been fourteen years since we left the river, but there are nights when I still feel that lovely sensation of gently rocking back and forth in my boat on the river as I drift off to sleep.

The Making of the Boat Basin

The 79th Street Boat Basin is umbilically linked to Riverside Park by its docks and gates that open to the park's promenade. The park itself starts at 72nd Street and runs along the Hudson from West 72nd Street into Harlem. In 2010, Riverside Park South was added. It starts at West 59th Street and connects to the rest of the park at 72nd Street. From my boat

I could see the seasonal change of the many trees in the park. When I first moved to the river in late October, I could see the trees in their autumnal reds, yellows, and oranges—markers of New York City in transition from the deep greens of summer to the gorgeous pigments of fall.

Before European contact, the area that became Riverside Park was dotted with sandy beaches. Deep forests ended at cliffs with streams pouring over them into the Hudson. In his book *Mannahatta: A Natural History of New York City*, Eric Sanderson writes that the Hudson River estuary is what helped this area become so biologically diverse. Sanderson describes the pivotal role that estuaries play in biodiversity, writing:

> History, geography, and climate all set Mannahatta up to be a biological success, but what makes Mannahatta wealthy beyond imagination is its crowning position atop an estuary. By definition, estuaries are the places where the land and sea come together, and the result is like currency, both productive and variable. Freshwater rivers, like the Hudson and the numerous streams that are her sources and tributaries, discharge nutrients to fertilize the water, and cut the saltwater with fresh flow. As the seasons turn, the amount of freshwater swells and diminishes, and as the days and nights pass, the tide rises and falls. The competing traffic of freshwater and saltwater and the washing of water over land creates a small sea in the glacially excavated harbor, with layers of warm ocean water lying on top of the cold, fresh stuff. Sea-grass beds take root where the water is shallow enough for light to reach the bottom, beaches and dunes form along the windward shore, and salt marshes thrive in protected corners. The estuary is the motor, the connector, the driver, the great winding way, the central place that gathers all the old neighborhoods together and makes the rest possible.[3]

When the Dutch and then the English invaded and drove the Indigenous people off of Manhattan Island, the ensuing period of colonization changed the environment in fundamental ways. In the 1840s, the New York Central Railroad built train tracks along the western shore of Manhattan, ultimately connecting Manhattan to Albany. By the 1850s, farms were built on land above the Hudson River that would become known as the Upper West Side and West Harlem. Gone, then, was the land filled with deep forests through which streams flowed and emptied into the Hudson. Gone was a shoreline dotted with beaches and rocky outcrops that overlooked the river. In place of these natural wonders were train tracks with train engines belching coal smoke and carrying cattle and pigs to market from farms north of the city.

While the creation of Central Park in the 1860s inspired the quick development of the Upper East Side, the urban transformation of the area west of Central Park was slower. In 1865, New York City's Parks Commissioner William R. Martin acquired 191 acres of farmland between West 72nd Street and 125th Street, hoping to beautify the land above the train tracks with a new park. By 1866, Andrew Haswell Green, a renowned urban planner and prominent leader of the Central Park Commission, presented the plan for Riverside Park to the New York State Legislature in Albany, which gave its approval. Green was the driving force behind uniting the five boroughs into New York City in 1898 and the visionary who chose Frederick Law Olmsted and Calvert Vaux's Greensward Plan to create Central Park. He also supported the creation of the American Museum of Natural History, the Bronx Zoo, the New York Public Library, and the Metropolitan Museum of Art, and he founded the American Scenic and Historic Preservation Society, which, as already mentioned, helped save the Palisades from destruction.[4]

Olmsted was chosen to create the new park above the river, and he designed the meandering Riverside Drive and the tree-lined sidewalk that hugged it from 72nd to 125th Streets. Between 1875 and 1910, landscape architect Vaux and horticulturist Samuel Parsons Jr. further developed Olmsted's work by creating a beautifully planted park based on the English gardening ideal of flowing curves that followed the river.

The Upper West Side continued to evolve, now cradled between Central Park and Riverside Park. But even with these beautification developments, the trains continued to disturb the area closest to the river with their noise and pollution. Enter Robert Moses, an ambitious idealist with an eye toward politics and planning. In his biography of Moses, Robert Caro describes the twenty-five-year-old's disgust as he stood on a bluff on Riverside Drive in 1914:

> Below him, along the edge of the river, was a wasteland, a wasteland six miles long, stretching from where he stood all the way north to 181st Street. The wasteland was named Riverside Park, [but] the "park" was nothing but a vast low-lying mass of dirt and mud. Running through its length was the

four-track bed of the New York Central, which lay in a right-of-way that had been turned over to the railroad by the city half a century before. Unpainted, rusting, jagged wire fences along the tracks barred the city from its water-front; in the whole six miles, there were exactly three bridges on which the tracks could be crossed and they led only to private boating clubs. . . . At 79th and 96th Streets untreated garbage mounded toward the sky; the San-itation Department used those areas as dumping grounds from which the garbage was transferred to scows, which towed it out to the open sea.[5]

As his power in the city grew, Moses was eager to correct this blight and realize his dream of a clean park. In early 1934, as the new parks commissioner of New York City, he started planning the West Side Improvement Project in earnest. To achieve his vision, Moses deter-mined it would be necessary to remove the shacks of the homeless men—mostly veterans of World War I—who had begun making homes along the river after being expelled from Washington, DC, following massive protests in 1932.

During those initial protests in the capital, nearly fifty thousand veter-ans formed encampments with their families in what became known as "Hoovervilles." These former soldiers had lost everything in the Great Depression, and they called for the government to pay their promised bonus money from their service during World War I—money that wouldn't come until 1945—that they needed to survive homelessness and jobless-ness. Eventually they were forced from the city by tear gas, bayonets, guns, and tanks at the behest of President Herbert Hoover and enforced by General Douglas MacArthur, Major Dwight Eisenhower, and Major George Patton.[6]

Many of the men who left Washington then moved to New York City—some building their shantytowns in Central Park and some along the Hudson. They built shacks from anything they could find, including old Broadway sets that had been thrown away. They were a proud group of men who once had jobs and who served their country in the war. The men named the community they created by the river Camp Thomas Paine after the author of *Common Sense*. The camp had almost one hundred shacks that lined the river along the West 70s. There was a large vegetable garden that helped feed the men. The community also received aid from wealthy neighbors—including Charles Schwab.[7]

Schwab was the former president of US Steel, founder of Bethlehem Steel, and a self-made millionaire. He had a mansion on land that extended from West 73rd to West 74th and from West End Avenue to Riverside Drive. (Now the apartment building known as the Schwab House sits on that property.) Still, he understood hardship. He had lost a great deal of money in the stock market crash of 1929, so he had empathy for the men living in shacks along the Hudson. He fed them and hired them for fifty cents a day to shovel his grounds in the winter.[8]

In April 1934, a determined and unsympathetic Moses gave the men less than a month to vacate their camp. On April 30, a day before the official eviction date, the Board of Aldermen (now the New York City Council), passed a resolution demanding that the order be rescinded. They accused Moses of "steam shovel government." Moses scoffed, calling the vote cheap politics, and responded: "How can we progress on the West Side Improvement without removing all encroachment along the river? I don't take their action seriously."[9]

The very next day, May 1, 1934, Camp Thomas Paine was bulldozed.[10]

With this "encroachment" removed, Moses was finally in position to expand the park to the river and start building a marina, playgrounds, and baseball fields. City, state, and federal government funding was available to put tens of thousands of jobless and hungry men to work building this infrastructure, and Moses scooped up that money to pay for the West Side Improvement Project. When all was completed, the ugly railroad tracks were covered by a beautiful new road, the Henry Hudson Parkway. The parkway connected Manhattan to Riverdale via a picturesque drive along the river. And at 79th Street, a marina was built.

Throughout the long new park were playgrounds, wading pools, tennis courts, ball fields, basketball courts, and running tracks. Tree-lined promenades were built on top of the covered railroad tracks. Facing the new marina and the Hudson, Moses built a decorative rotunda designed with Guastavino tiled arches and a large circular fountain created by twenty-four spouting bronze turtles. Staircases curved around both sides of the rotunda, connecting the upper park to the river and the 79th Street Boat Basin. Moses also added 131 acres of fill that allowed New Yorkers to reach their river, now free of the noisy, smelly railroad cars.

Forty years later, in 1980, the year our son was born, Riverside Park was designated a scenic landmark by the New York City Landmarks Preservation Commission.

Moorings

I have a photo of my mother, taken by my father in 1940. She is sitting next to his cousin on the edge of the West 79th Street Rotunda fountain. She is twenty, newly married, and looking fancy and beautiful in a white stole, with a gorgeous costume jewelry necklace. A wide-brimmed straw hat with a long black grosgrain ribbon hangs from her arm. The ribbon floats down next to her crossed legs. That same day my mother took a photo of my father and his cousin, leaning against the Boat Basin

Figure 4. Adele Wohl, Leslie's mother (*right*), and a relative sitting on the ledge of the newly built West 79th Street Rotunda fountain, Riverside Park, New York City, 1940.

railing, a glimpse of the river and boats behind them. Here they were starting their lives together as husband and wife visiting the exact place I would meet my husband-to-be thirty-five years later: the 79th Street Boat Basin.

The first time I saw my neighbor Jim Nishiura he was coming home from work. Our boats were maybe two feet apart, separated by a narrow wooden dock called a finger dock. The scene is engraved in my mind: A handsome man in glasses, carrying a briefcase, steps up onto his houseboat's deck. He turns to the right and looks directly at me. I wonder, Is he Hawaiian? He looks Asian. He is tall and muscular. We take each other in—no smiles, no nods, no waves. Then he moves out of sight into his boat.

Figure 5. Howard Wohl, Leslie's father (*right*) and a relative leaning against the railing of the 79th Street Boat Basin with the Hudson River behind them, Riverside Park, New York City, 1940.

As I later learned, Jim was not Hawaiian but Japanese American. Jim's grandfather, Shinzaburo, and great uncle, Gentaro, had emigrated from Japan to Hawaii in the early 1900s and briefly took jobs in shipbuilding. The work was familiar to them because their father, Tsurukichi, was a skilled craftsman, and the Nishiura family ran their own lumber mill in Kehara, a small mountain village in Japan.

After a short time in Hawaii, the brothers moved to Northern California, where they were joined, over time, by other family members. They gained recognition for their refined carpentry skills and aesthetic sensibility, and across the opening decades of the twentieth century, the Nishiura Brothers Construction Company built many prominent public structures in San Jose's Japantown.

The brothers also helped construct the Japanese Pavilion at the 1915 Panama-Pacific International Exhibition in San Francisco. After the exhibition closed, part of the Japanese Pavilion was relocated to the Japanese Tea Garden in Golden Gate Park. In 1937, they completed the San Jose Buddhist Church Betsuin, a temple still used by the Japanese American community today. In 1939, they were hired to build the Golden Gate International Exposition on Treasure Island in the San Francisco Bay. This long list of achievements by the Nishiura brothers continued right up to the outbreak of war with Japan and beyond.

Figure 6. Jim's brothers Takao, Eizo, and Togo Nishiura (*left to right*) stand by the newly constructed San Jose Buddhist Church Betsuin, built by their grandfather and great uncle, Shinzaburo and Gentaro Nishiura, 1938.

In 2019, Jim and I, our son Jonah, our daughter-in-law Gina Auletta, and our granddaughter Aya, spent two weeks in Japan. We went to Kehara to find the family cemetery. Jim was sure that the ancestral home was long gone, but we discovered it sitting on a slope overlooking a narrow river valley: a large farmhouse that was hundreds of years old with a decorative tiled roof. The owner is a distant cousin. He knew that most of the family lived in California, but he was not in touch with anyone, and none of Jim's family knew of his existence. Since then, family members have traveled to Kehara to visit the Nishiura cousin and the ancestral family home.

Following the attack on Pearl Harbor, President Franklin D. Roosevelt issued Executive Order 9066, and all the people of Japanese descent living on the West Coast were rounded up and shipped to internment camps. Jim's parents, older siblings (there were five at that time: Takao, Togo, Eizo, Yukiko, and infant Frank), grandparents, great aunts and uncles—his entire family—were taken to the Heart Mountain Relocation Center in Wyoming. During their incarceration, Shinzaburo and Gentaro built three exquisite *butsudan*, elaborately carved family shrines. One of these

Figure 7. Japanese internment camp barracks, looking toward Heart Mountain, Wyoming, winter 1941.

is currently housed in the Smithsonian Institution in Washington, DC. Jim was born in the camp on November 1, 1944. The last son, Alfred, was born after the war in 1950.

Jim's father Shingo had immigrated to America in 1915, following his father and uncles. As an artist, he studied at the California School of Fine Arts, but after starting a family, he became a gardener to earn a living. It was one of the few jobs open to Japanese men during the early part of the century.

Shingo spent time botanizing and drawing and painting the flowering plants that thrived in the area. He and other artists in the relocation camp started their own chapter of the Art Students League of Los Angeles, and they taught art to children and adults.

Shingo and his wife had seven children over a period of twenty years, so money was tight. Gardening is backbreaking labor, and I remember Jim telling me about how hard his father worked. When the children turned

Figure 8. Heart Mountain wildflowers botanical painting by Shingo Nishiura, 1942.

Figure 9. Shingo Nishiura (*seated in center*), teaching an art class at Heart Mountain Relocation Center, Wyoming, 1943.

Figure 10. Heart Mountain internment camp painting by Shingo Nishiura, 1943.

Figure 11. Baby Jim Nishiura, brother Frank Nishiura, grandmother Tani Nishiura, Heart Mountain Relocation Center, Wyoming, 1945.

five and were old enough to help, Jim's father would have them join him on the weekends in the gardens of his clients—weeding, pruning, raking, mowing, all the typical tasks. Jim loved rainy weekends because they meant he didn't have to toil in a garden.

As the Nishiura children grew up and moved away, they continued to send money to help the family. Takao became an architect. Togo and Eizo both became mathematics professors. Yukiko, known as Patricia, became a teacher. Frank became an engineer, and the youngest, Al, also became an architect.

Jim worked with his father until he went to college, where he studied biology. Eventually he obtained his PhD and did a postdoc fellowship in genetics, before landing a teaching job at Brooklyn College, City University of New York. He moved from Seattle with his first wife, Leah, and they came to live on a boat in Manhattan. That is how Jim became my next-door neighbor, with only the slimmest of docks between our boats.

Jim's marriage fell apart, and Leah left. Jim and I, once just friends and neighbors, became more than that as we fell in love and eventually married. When I learned about Jim's gardening experience, I told him about my first attempt to grow plants. I was six and very determined. With allowance money that I had saved over many weeks, I went to Woolworth's. I looked for the most colorful flower images on the packets and finally chose a package with mixed seeds.

Figure 12. Leslie Day and young neighbor Annick Murat on a houseboat deck garden, 1998.

Back at home, I asked my mother to help me plant them. She loved her indoor plants and had them everywhere, so in my mind she was a wonderful gardener. Yet, when I asked her to help me plant my seeds, she said she was too busy. She gave me a spoon and a cup of water. She told me to go outside, dig a hole, put the seeds in, cover the hole, and pour in the water.

Out I went on that hot summer day and tried to dig a hole in the dry, compacted, urban soil of Queens. Then, day after day, I checked the spot, watching and waiting for my flowers to emerge. But weeks passed and nothing grew. That would have been the end of my passion for gardening had I not met Jim.

When Jim heard this story, he got some wood and built three long boxes. He put them on our deck and filled them with soil, vermiculite, manure, and bonemeal. Then we planted seeds together, and by the summer we had six-foot-tall sunflowers. It was twenty-six years after my disappointing first venture into gardening, but I had finally found someone to teach and help me.

After that I started planting a full container garden on our deck. My neighbors were also serious gardeners: Meg Berlin had a gorgeous garden of native plants on her deck, and Kazumi Hayama had a thriving vegetable garden on hers. My neighbor Josh Bloomgarden had huge sunflowers

Figure 13. Neighbor Josh Bloomgarden with his banjo, sunflowers, and morning glories on his houseboat, 79th Street Boat Basin, 1992.

and morning glory vines climbing up and over the railings of his houseboat. All up and down C dock—one of the original docks of the marina and one of the largest—there were beautifully planted wooden containers. And every summer, the marina bloomed.

Bonding

For most of my life, I didn't want children. I remember coming home on the 79th Street crosstown bus one day with a screaming toddler sitting behind me and thinking: That child is a ball and chain.

But as my relationship with Jim grew, and as I began to trust his love, thoughtfulness, and care—things I had never experienced before—suddenly all I could think about was having a baby. I was enchanted by babies asleep in strollers, babies held in their mothers' arms, babies held against their mothers' chests in carriers. I was enthralled by seeing babies everywhere.

I got pregnant in 1979. Once I knew the baby would be a boy, I started imagining what our son—half Japanese, half Ashkenazi Jew—would look like. I remember glimpsing a beautiful young man on the corner of

Figure 14. Jim Nishiura and baby Jonah, 79th Street Boat Basin, 1981.

72nd Street and Broadway who looked like he might be partially Asian. I thought with amazement, That is what he might look like!

While I absolutely loved being pregnant, my nausea and the boat's rocking made for a tough combination in the first three months. Once the difficulties of the first trimester subsided, I started to fully relish my pregnancy. The comfortable rhythm I had established in my second trimester was eventually disrupted at month five. On a cold late February day, following a night of heavy snow, I walked out onto the deck, and my cat Nessim followed me. I picked him up, looked around, and said, "Oh! How beautiful!"

Then, I took one step and immediately slipped on an icy patch. Down I fell and rolled toward the edge of the deck. My first instinct was to put Nessim down so he wouldn't fall into the river. In the seconds it took to let go of my cat, I probably could have grabbed onto something instead, but I never thought to do that. Into the drink I went.

The tide was high that morning, and the freezing water was deep enough that I couldn't stand on the riverbed. Underwater, I could see the V-shaped hull of our houseboat. I swam to the surface and grabbed the dock, but I had no leverage. I couldn't pull myself out.

My neighbor across the dock was just leaving for work and saw me struggling. She screamed for Jim, who came rushing out. With a super-human strength born of adrenaline, he reached down with one arm and pulled me up and out of the river. After rushing me to a hot shower, Jim called my obstetrician and told him what happened. I was terrified that being in the cold water had harmed the baby, but the doctor reassured Jim that we had nothing to worry about—the baby was bathed in warm amniotic fluid.

That spring my neighbors in the Boat Basin held a surprise baby shower for me on Mother's Day. It was a beautiful Sunday morning in May, and all the apple trees along the river were in pink-blossomed splendor. I felt so cared for surrounded by my neighbors' warmth and generosity.

In July 1980, the summer our son Jonah was born, the city baked in a weeks-long heat wave with over 100 degree temperatures. We never had air conditioning in our more than thirty-six years of living on a boat, and during intense heat waves like that one, we suffered along with all New Yorkers. I remember staying on the shady side of the street whenever we went away from the boat and even carrying an umbrella to protect my baby's skin.

Living near water means being cooler in the summer than inland and being *much* cooler in the winter. In summer, water molecules absorb heat from the air, cooling the air. During the day, the land is warmer than the water as it heats up more quickly. As the warm air rises from the land, the cooler air over the river flows over the land, creating a river or sea breeze. Yet, the nights are cool because the breezes start moving the opposite way, from land to water. At night, the land cools more quickly than the water, so the warm air over the water rises and is replaced by land breezes, bringing lovely, gentle winds that rocked our boat and us to sleep.

Water possesses magical properties, which are based on powerful hydrogen bonds. Each water molecule is made up of two atoms of hydrogen—the tiniest of all atoms—and one atom of oxygen, a larger, magnetically stronger atom. These three atoms are covalently bound together because they share electrons. The oxygen atom is bigger and stronger, and it pulls more of the electrons toward it, making it slightly negative. Think of sharing a blanket with your bigger sibling who tugs it close to them—that is oxygen. The little hydrogen atoms then become slightly positive because their electrons have moved closer to the oxygen. Illustrations of a water molecule make it look like Mickey Mouse's head. The round face is the oxygen, and the two small ears are the hydrogen atoms. As liquid water moves, the slightly positive hydrogen atoms in the molecule—Mickey's ears—are attracted to nearby negative oxygen atoms in the water—Mickey's face— forming hydrogen bonds, and this is what holds water molecules together in our bodies or as they move against gravity from the soil to the leaves in trees or stay locked together in oceans, lakes, streams, ponds, puddles, or a glass of water. This force is called cohesion, and it is what makes life on earth possible. This magnetic attraction, this bond between hydrogen and oxygen, is the key to life. And when looking at a body of water, it is what we see, and feel, as beauty.

When Jonah was only three months old, I enrolled us in a mommy-and-me swim class at the West Side YMCA. If you're going to live on a boat, you'd better be able to swim. I wanted him to learn to swim, be unafraid, and to love water.

Jonah was in swim classes for the first four years of his life, but it was only after a mishap on our way home from school that I finally began to trust his ability to swim. We were walking down the dock when Jonah had an itchy nose and reached to scratch it. As he scratched, he closed his eyes and proceeded to walk right off the dock and into the river. He bobbed up and yelled, "Mama!"

As calmly as I could, I said, "Swim," and he swam to me. I didn't freak out because I didn't want him to. My heart was pounding, but I was so proud of him.

Raising a child on a boat has its challenges. How do you keep little children from falling into the river? The dock was like the busy street outside everyone else's home: a place you never let your small child roam unattended. Having a community of people made all the difference. We relied on our neighbors for almost everything—babysitting, dog walking, grocery shopping if we were sick or injured, and moral support on trips to the vet when our cat or bird or dog was sick. When I first moved to the marina, one of my neighbors told me he knew who I was dating by seeing who was walking my dog.

Extended Family

The Boat Basin was a close-knit community. We had dinners together and celebrated birthdays, weddings, baby and bridal showers, and holidays, as well as funerals and memorials when one of our own died.

As more children grew up at the marina, Halloween became special for families. Kids went boat to boat with their plastic pumpkin pails and bags, holding a parent's hand and getting helped onto boats where they were treated to candy and apples.

For Sukkot, the Jewish harvest festival in October, several neighbors built sukkahs on top of their houseboats. Sukkahs have three walls and a roof made of leaves or branches to shade you, but they are open enough to look up at the stars.

Figure 15. A bearded Jim Nishiura (*left*) with neighbors on a houseboat deck, 1996.

For Thanksgiving, a group of men, women, babies, adolescents, and seniors in their seventies and eighties would go to Dallas BBQ on West 72nd Street and have a feast together.

For the winter holidays, there was a competition among the boats to see who could create the most beautiful light display. Trees were decorated and placed on dinghies. A small group of us, named by our neighbor Ed Bacon as the "Not Ready for Prime Time Carolers," went from dock to dock singing Christmas and Hanukkah songs. When we got too cold, we'd go inside someone's boat for brandy or whatever else was on hand. On New Year's Eve, neighbors from the Netherlands continued their country's tradition of creating a midnight bonfire with Christmas trees in the ball field outside the marina gate.

Spring and summer holidays were also celebrated at the marina. The Fourth of July was the biggest celebration of all. My first Fourth of July at the marina was in 1976, the Bicentennial of the United States. There was a huge celebration on the Hudson. We watched the Grand Parade of Sailing Ships all day long. Ships hundreds of feet long with enormous, colorful sails cruised up and down the river, carrying the flags of their countries.

The Macy's fireworks were held on the Hudson on barges right off the marina. We all had friends and family sit on our decks and watch the

Figure 16. Leslie on the Hudson during the Grand Parade of Sailing Ships, July 1976.

fireworks explode over our heads. The Riverside Park promenade was packed with thousands of people, and the river was filled with boats of every size, from dinghies to yachts. It was spectacular.

Neighbors

My dearest friends at the marina were like family: always there when we needed them, when we wanted to celebrate a major life event, and when we were hurt, sick, or lonely. Doug Hynes walked our dogs, fed our cats, helped find our lost bird, Paulie, and fed all the little songbirds, ducks, geese, and swans. Raquel and Werner Buhrer were devoted to our son Jonah and were there at every major event of our lives. Ray Stephens was like a brother to Jim and me and an uncle to Jonah, always there to make us laugh and, as a physician's assistant, there to help when we were injured. Jane Clegg, who, as president of the Hudson Harbor Preservation Association, defended our right to exist. My brilliant friends Meg Berlin, photographer and gardener, Jane White, director of education at ABC News Interactive, Leslee Smoke, child psychologist, and Cindy Kane, artist, enriched my life.

We depend on the people we see and who see us every day. We notice when they don't appear, when they seem upset, or when they are excited about something in their lives. Living on a boat on the mighty Hudson River with extreme weather, storms, fires, and sinkings makes you truly dependent on the kindness and keen observance of those nearest you. Several of my neighbors stand out because of their dramatic life stories.

Michele Capozzi and Simone Di Bagno

Michele Capozzi and Simone Di Bagno were friends and filmmakers from Italy who moved to the Boat Basin in 1978. They lived on E dock. Michele was a filmmaker and tour guide of New York City's underground culture. Simone was an award-winning documentarian and artist. He worked for the United Nations for twenty years, covering the Khmer Rouge in Cambodia, the military coups in Burma, and other war-torn areas of the world.

I asked Simone what had inspired him to work for the UN, and he told me about his family in Italy. His grandfather had been a much-decorated general in the Italian army in World War I. After fighting in the colonial wars in Africa in the 1930s, he retired just as World War II began. When the Germans occupied Italy, he joined the Italian military resistance to the Nazis. He was betrayed, arrested, tortured, and then executed in an infamous massacre in Rome in 1944.

Simone's father was a captain in the famous cavalry regiment, "Genova Cavalleria," and participated in the occupation of "Free France"—the southern coastal strip of France that runs from the Spanish to the Italian borders. During that time, the regiment sheltered the Jewish populations of the area. The Italians hid them from the Germans for a whole year, moving them from city to city until the end of the war.

The European wars took a terrible toll on Simone's family, including his uncle who was killed in World War II. For Simone's family, "the most telling of the tragedy of Italy at the time was that my grandfather was killed by the Germans, and his son, my uncle, was killed in North Africa by the British." This family history of loss made him want to work toward peace. While Simone worked at the UN, he lived at the marina year-round, except when he was traveling the world.

On a cold, windless night in February, I was walking around the marina to look at the full moon. Calm water, unruffled by wind, is a perfect mirror, reflecting the sky, clouds, trees, and buildings. At night, the reflections are even more mesmerizing: The lights along the river's edge on the New Jersey side and the Manhattan side are perfectly reflected—even on freezing winter nights.

I stopped to talk to Michele. We were standing looking south toward Midtown, watching the moon and its mirror image on the glazed river, when a passing boat caused a series of waves. The river was covered in a thin layer of ice, and as the waves moved toward the dock, the icy undulations reflected the moon at the crest of each unbroken wave. Michele and I laughed and hugged, filled with wonder at the sight—seen only once in the almost four decades that I lived there.

In 2008, Ed Bacon, a major community activist for decades, started circulating a marina newsletter called the *Boat Basin BULLetin*, where he told the stories of some of our neighbors.[11] When he asked Simone what attracted him to the Boat Basin, he replied, "In Mexico, there's an artist colony resort, a Pueblo Magico, a 'Magical Village.' The Boat Basin is one of the few magical villages of the world."

Michele and Simone had a wooden boat, *The Excalibur*, that sank many times. After their boat sank one time too many, Simone finally bought a boat with a fiberglass hull and made it into a floating palace, decorating it with lights and textiles and flags he had collected from his trips around the world. Now retired, he spends spring and summer in Rome and winters in Baja, where he lives in a shack on the beach and paints. Sweet Michele died at the age of seventy-seven in his native Genoa.

Nobuhiro "Yama" Yamauchi

Nobuhiro Yamauchi, known to all his neighbors as Yama, arrived at the marina on a tiny sailboat. I had heard that he sailed to Tahiti from Japan and somehow made his way to New York and the Boat Basin. Yama was an artist in the fullest sense of that word. He spent all his daylight hours sculpting or painting. His art was his life.

He would find fallen tree trunks in Riverside Park, drag them back to the marina, and prop them up against the ball field's chain-link fence next to the allée of crab apple trees. He carved them, creating totem pole–like

Figure 17. Nobuhiro "Yama" Yamauchi carving totem poles from fallen basswood trees outside the marina along the ball field fence, 1990.

structures. He told me his favorite tree to carve was the linden tree because the wood was soft. He said it cut like butter.

Yama had no car, and once the Japanese market Mitsue opened across the river in Edgewater, New Jersey, he would walk north along the river, over the George Washington Bridge, then south along the Jersey side of the river for several miles to shop at Mitsue. Then he'd walk back with his groceries. It probably entailed ten miles of walking each way, but that is how he stocked up on his food.

In the summer of 2001, Yama went back to Japan for a visit. He booked his return flight for September. When he arrived shortly after the attacks on 9/11, he was asked to show his green card or citizenship papers, and he did not have either. He was sent back to Japan, and we never saw him again.

I have described only a few people from our unique community, but there were so many over the years. Some moved away and some passed away, but their generosity and compassion, the joy in being with them and sharing our lives, will always remain.

Ducks, Geese, and Other Friends

The Boat Basin community extended beyond people. Over the years, I came to know the wildlife that made homes in the area. The mallard ducks would begin their mating during the winter with foreplay that included mutual head bobbing. If the females weren't interested, they would take off and fly around the marina, often with a cloud of males close behind. Once in a great while, a female mallard would have a mate for life that would stay with her during breeding season as she sat on her eggs for thirty days. After her eggs hatched, he would help her protect their ducklings.

Most females would be alone in caring for their young, nine or more ducklings at a time. Much to our horror, these ducklings would often get separated from their families and peep and peep for hours, lonely and lost. The sound of those lost babies broke our hearts.

Just as we would lend care to the humans of our community, my family and others occasionally took in some lost ducklings and raised them until they were mature enough to fend for themselves. Otherwise, fast-moving currents would carry them away, and slowly but surely their numbers would dwindle.

The ducklings that were protected by both parents had a much better chance of survival. They would swim in a straight line with dad in the front and mom in the back. The Canada geese fared much better because they always mate for life, and both parents raise the young. Like the ducks, the geese swam the river with the male in front followed by his eight or nine goslings and the female in the rear, ready to round up and protect any errant babies.

There was one duck, probably a hybrid mallard, that was named Henry by one of our neighbors. Henry looked just like a male mallard, except he was huge, almost twice as large as a typical male, with a massive, round, emerald head, bright orange feet, and a large yellow bill. He was gorgeous and friendly. He'd hop up on the dock and follow us around, always with a greeting or a farewell in front of our boat. He also adopted ducklings if they got lost.

When I kayaked, Henry would swim alongside my boat, quacking his unusual and easily identifiable quack—a deeper and louder sound than the other males. Henry hung around for at least ten years, and then one day he was gone. Raccoons were suspected. They visited the marina at night and explored the rocks along the river's edge where Henry liked to sleep. Those of us who loved Henry grieved for him as we would any other member of our community.

We also fed the geese throughout the winter. There was one Canada goose that Jim named Hurtwing because of a broken wing that trailed along the top of the river as she swam. Hurtwing managed to live for years without ever flying. She swam to the people who fed her. If the swans came by, she would hide on the other side of our boat until they left. She was sweet and gentle. She never paired up with a male or had a family, but her fortitude—her appearance day after day, year after year—was miraculous to so many of us at the marina. We were her family, and we took care of her as she nurtured us with her beautiful presence.

There were a few pairs of geese that stayed near the marina, laid their eggs on top of pilings, and brought their young to us as little yellow fluff balls. The mother would sit on her nest for a month, while the male swam around the piling, protecting her. Once all her babies had hatched, the

Figure 18. Neighbor Clodagh Green greeting Henry the duck, 2005.

Figure 19. The Canada goose, Hurtwing, swimming next to Leslie's boat, 1999.

Figure 20. Canada geese goslings huddled together for warmth.
Copyright © Beth Bergman.

mother would hop off the nest, followed by the goslings, one at time, as they jumped at least twelve feet down to the river.

Geese, swan, and duck babies are precocial. They are born fully feathered with their eyes open, and they are able to swim, walk, and eat on their own. However, their feathers are down and offer little protection from the cold, so at night they would come up on land in the park and gather under their mother's outstretched wings for warmth.

Swans, like geese and some ducks, mate for life. Divorce is very rare, but mates will seek out new mates when theirs has died. Our area has two species of swans: the native, though not commonly seen, tundra swan, and the commonly seen, introduced by colonists hundreds of years ago and now naturalized, mute swan. The first time I saw a pair of mute swans was during the nor'easter of 1992, when the wind was howling, and the rain didn't stop for three days. I saw them the first morning of the storm, flying madly back and forth over the marina. The storm was brutal, and

Figure 21. Leslie feeding swans from Cindy Kane and Doron Katzman's houseboat, 1994. Photo by Cindy Kane.

the boats offered some protection from the wind, so the swans stayed and made the marina their home during the winter of 1992–93.

They were exquisite, and they trusted those of us who fed them and talked to them. They would announce their presence with a soft purring sound. When they left in March, I felt grateful that the storm had brought them to us, but I missed them. I was sure we wouldn't see them again.

The summer passed, and in September I got an excited, happy call from my friend Cindy Kane, who lived on A dock—the northernmost dock in the marina. "Leslie, the swans are back, and they're headed your way!"

I looked out my window, and there were seven swans! I saw two adults and five cygnets—young, gray-colored swans, almost as big as their parents. I was overjoyed. They stayed at the marina until spring, when the cygnets' gray feathers were replaced with white. They all left again in March, but the parents returned with new cygnets every fall for six years.

It was gifts like these—the community of people and nature—that changed my life forever.

Chapter 3

STUDENT, TEACHER

River Lessons

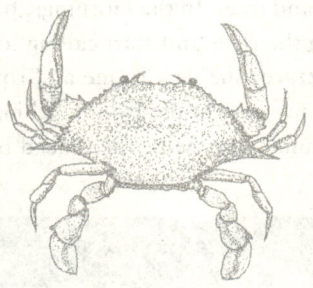

Even as a very young child, I was a student of the natural world. I collected rocks of different sizes, textures, and colors and checked out geology books from the library in the hopes of understanding more about what I had found. I brought home seashells from the beach and went to the American Museum of Natural History to try to identify them. I collected all kinds of beetles and other insects and kept them in my room so I could observe their behavior. I loved looking at their colors: ladybugs, lacewings, Japanese beetles, potato bugs, and milkweed bugs—they were all beautiful to me then. They still are.

While I had an abundant curiosity about the natural world, my mother—terrified of all invertebrates—was not enthused about my passions. And without adults in my life to bolster my interests in the natural world, my knowledge of its intricacies remained limited for a long time. I knew the difference between a pigeon and a sparrow or between a blue jay and a starling, but many of the birds and other animals that populated the city passed me by without names.

That all changed one day in 1983. I was walking our two dogs around the ball field next to the marina, scattering leftover seed from my neighbor Werner Buhrer's eighty-year-old pet parrot, Bobo. I was expecting only the usual takers when, suddenly, a gorgeous little bird flew up to me. She was about nine inches long and tawny brown, with a red crest and a red beak. She followed me around the ballfield and ate the seed along with the pigeons and sparrows. I had to know what she was. I borrowed a field guide from a friend and looked her up. A female northern cardinal!

For the next three years, she accompanied me on my daytime dog walks. Twice a day and through every season, she perched near me on park benches, shrubs, and trees. In the mornings, before sunup, she would sit on the railing along the river and start calling to me—*Tsip! Tsip!*

Once, during a blizzard, she flew to me as I rounded the traffic circle above the rotunda on my way home from teaching at the 92nd Street Y. I ran to the boat for sunflower seeds, then raced back to the park where

Figure 22. Female cardinal, *Cardinalis cardinalis*, Leslie's muse.
Copyright © Beth Bergman.

she, along with blue jays, house sparrows, starlings, and pigeons, all waited for food. I cleared the snow away from the base of a large tree and scattered the seeds. The hungry birds flew down to the ground and fed as I stood there, watching and feeling love and gratitude toward this cardinal for including me in her life and the lives of my avian neighbors.

After three years of her daily companionship, on a lovely spring day, a dazzling red cardinal showed up—a gorgeous male—and she flew away with him. I looked for her over many weeks, walking the park from 72nd Street to 96th Street, asking every female cardinal I saw, "Is it you?" But none of them looked up or followed me.

Growing Things

I never saw that cardinal again, but she changed my life. She reawakened the curiosity I had possessed as a young child, as a collector and observer and lover of the natural world. I wanted to know the name of every bird, tree, flower, mushroom, fish, crab, snail, and slug in the park and in the river, along the streets, and in the ponds, lakes, and streams of the city. I wanted to immerse myself in studying the lives and relationships of the plants and animals of my world. Now, as an adult, I could educate myself.

I went back to school and finished my undergraduate degree. Soon after, I enrolled in the early childhood master's degree program at Bank Street College of Education, and I started teaching nursery school.

I started teaching pre-K at the 92nd Street Y, then at the Heschel School on West 89th Street, followed by six years at the Calhoun Lower School on West 74th Street, where I found myself bringing more and more animals and plants into my classroom. The Calhoun School was between Central Park and Riverside Park, so my students and I were able to make weekly field trips to these two historic parks to look at the plants and animals living there. We also started growing vegetables in the classroom. I created a curriculum around the children's book *Stone Soup*. My students brought in vegetables to make soup. We cut the vegetables, germinated the seeds, and planted the seedlings, creating a *Stone Soup*–style garden in our classroom.

I gave my four-year-old students lima beans to soak overnight in water. Soaking softened the hard seed coat, or testa, so that we could more easily open them up the next day. Once we opened the bean, we looked inside at the baby leaves, or plumule, and the embryonic root, which is called the radicle. We also made germination bags, placing soaked seeds from our vegetables inside plastic baggies with wet paper towels that kept the seeds moist. Then we hung the bags on the south-facing windows of our classroom and watched over the next few days as the plant embryos emerged from the seeds. First, the baby root grew down, then the shoot emerged, growing up against gravity toward the light. The leaves emerged green and photosynthesized in the sunlight. Finally, we planted the seedlings in moist soil and over a couple of months watched them grow and flower, producing seed pods of their own.

Around the same time that we were germinating seeds in my pre-K classroom, one of my husband's colleagues at Brooklyn College found box turtle eggs buried in his backyard in Flatbush. He incubated them in his lab and found himself with three baby box turtles. When he passed away, Jim and I took the turtles. I brought one of them into my classroom, and the children named him Tommy.

We also had frogs, toads, and tadpoles in my class. My husband would liberate frogs slated for dissection in the biology department, and I collected tadpoles from our pond in the Catskills where we had a tiny A-frame cabin. I don't remember where I got a crayfish that lived in an aquarium in the classroom, but we had one of those too. I'd come into my classroom each morning, and the first thing I'd see was the crayfish waving its arms to get my attention for food. Once I put some food in the tank, the crayfish went about its life and wouldn't wave again until the next morning when I entered the classroom and turned on the lights.

Surrounding myself and the children with plants and animals made me happy. Learning about the physical world, especially the visible living world of plants and animals is one of life's greatest gifts for me, and I learned that the children felt the same way. They bonded with the classroom animals, and they bonded with the plants they were growing from seed. We fell in love with our box turtle, tadpoles, frogs, and crayfish. And there was always more to learn, for me as well as for my young students. We all wanted to keep the animals and the plants healthy and happy. It was then I realized that I wanted to teach science.

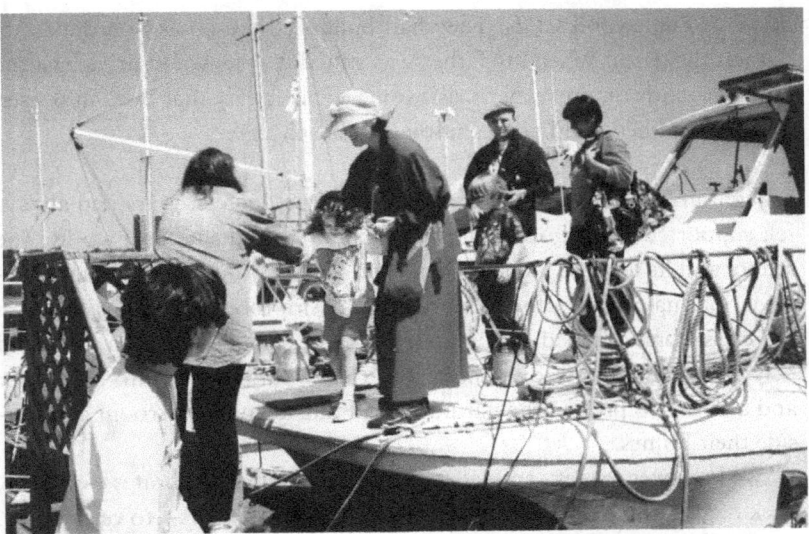

Figure 23. Leslie (*standing, with hat*) with her pre-K Calhoun class visiting her boat, 1993.

I enrolled in a doctoral program in science education at Teachers College, Columbia University, and got a job teaching middle school science at The Elisabeth Morrow School in Englewood, New Jersey.

The school sits on fourteen acres of land with gardens, a lovely wood, and a stream. The buildings and its grounds are rich with history. The main building had been the home and estate of the Dwight Morrow family, whose daughter Anne married Charles Lindbergh and came to that house to live with her parents in 1932 after the disappearance and murder of her baby. The family built a school for their other daughter, Elisabeth Morrow, who had gone to Europe in the 1920s to study the "kindergarten" movement, which was founded by Frederich Froebel on the belief that teachers of young children should use "music, nature study, stories, and dramatic play."[1] Elisabeth's school, which she called the Little School, was added to the Morrow family grounds.[2]

Teaching at the school brought back some of my own family history as well. Each day my commute took me up the Henry Hudson Parkway from the Boat Basin, to the George Washington Bridge, then to the Palisades Parkway, where I'd pass the estate gates surrounding my childhood home in Englewood Cliffs. They had bulldozed the houses on the estate but left the gates. When my father was still alive, we would drive past the estate grounds on our way to visit some of his family that lived in Bergen County, and he would point out the gates each time.

I taught at The Elisabeth Morrow School for seventeen years and always felt supported in my goal to introduce children to the natural world. The school and its leaders, Stephen Jones and then David Lowry, and my principal, Germaine DiPaolo, supported my desire to have animals living in the classroom. I hoped that by having them in our classroom, it would help the children develop connections that would evolve into a love for and a desire to protect the natural world outside our classroom and outside their homes.

We had over seventy animals that ranged from invertebrates—crickets, stick bugs, millipedes, caterpillars, butterflies, and spiders—to vertebrates. We had birds, five snakes, numerous turtles, frogs, toads, salamanders, chinchillas, rabbits, hamsters, mice, rats, guinea pigs, and a ferret named Beyoncé by her former nine-year-old owner. We also had an indoor koi pond and tanks filled with fish and aquatic invertebrates I'd collect from the river. Many of the animals were former pets that were no longer wanted. I never said no. All were welcome. Some of the children would arrive early in the morning or stay after school to help care for them. My classroom was a peaceable kingdom.

One year, my husband and I adopted a rescue terrier mix that we named Sadie, after my grandmother. Sadie came to school with me each day. That made my classroom just like my home. With animals from the Hudson, my dog, and animals my students loved and helped care for, the classroom was a haven. When students were upset, they'd come to the science room for solace.

I remember a boy named Chris who was yelled at by a teacher during rehearsal for the fifth grade play *Charlie and the Chocolate Factory*. Frustrated and humiliated, he ran into my classroom crying. He grabbed Tommy the box turtle from his tank, sat in the rocking chair holding him against his chest, and rocked back and forth. Then he stopped, stood up, thanked me, handed me Tommy, and went back to the play.

Figure 24. Leslie in her classroom at The Elisabeth Morrow School, holding Honey the rabbit, one of the seventy animals living in her classroom, 2006.

Figure 25. Leslie and Sadie kayaking on the Hudson, 2007.

Parents would tell me how their children were not only overcoming fears but were also becoming more interested in the natural world. They wanted to learn about the trees and birds in their backyards and the plants and animals they were seeing on their vacations. Their eyes were opening to the beauty and knowledge that nature offers.

When I taught the river to my fifth grade students, I used *The Hudson: An Illustrated Guide to the Living River.*[3] Stephen Stanne, the principal author, was director of education for the sailing sloop, the *Clearwater*, for decades, and until his retirement, he was director of education for the Hudson River Estuary Program, which is run by the New York Department of Environmental Conservation.

Together, my students and I learned about the moon and the tides from *The Hudson*. We learned that the gathering of water remains below the moon as the earth continues to spin on its axis and that the swelling is largest when the sun, moon, and earth are aligned. This occurs when there is a full moon, when the earth is between the sun and the moon, or during a new moon, which is when the moon is between the earth and the sun and the side facing us is dark.

High tides are the highest and low tides are at their lowest during these alignments. Although the sun is huge, it is so far away that it doesn't have as much pull, but when it is exactly 180 degrees opposite the moon, it supplements the gravitational pull of the full or new moon, causing what's called "spring tides." This term has nothing to do with the spring season but refers to tides springing forward.

The opposite of the spring tide is called the neap tide, when the moon is between its first and last quarter and is at a right angle to the sun. "Neap" is from an old Anglo-Saxon word that means "without power."[4] At neap tide, the gravitational pull is less, and high and low tides are not as extreme.

Roughly six hours after high tide, the Hudson and the entire Atlantic coast comes out of the moon-driven gravitational bulge. The tide ebbs (or moves out to sea) and reaches its low tide point.

At the Boat Basin, that meant dead low tide. The marina was last dredged in the 1960s and was so silted in that at low tide the boats sat on the river bottom. Some boats with deep, V-shaped hulls listed over to their sides. Looking out at dead low tide, I would see thousands of small eastern mudsnails, *Tritia obsoleta*, crawling over the muck, feeding on the algae and detritus lying in the riverbed, leaving long, silvery trails behind them. As the tide moved in, these native delicate mollusks, with darkly banded spiral shells, simply continued with their lives. They are omnivores, feeding on phytoplankton, dead fish, crustaceans, and tiny worms.

At dead low tide, incredulous passersby would yell from the shore promenade, "Where did the water go?" or "Did someone pull the plug?" Six hours later, the earth would rotate into the other bulge, and the tide and tidal currents would flow back into the Basin. "A rising tide lifts all boats" is a sure thing on the river.

A Little History

The river didn't always move both north and south, depending on ocean tides. To understand the Hudson, you have to look at its history before it was connected to the Atlantic Ocean and learn what happened afterward.

From 2.5 million years ago to roughly 13,000 years ago, the Laurentide Ice Sheet, in places two miles thick, covered millions of square miles over what is today Canada and the northern United States during the Pleistocene Epoch—the Ice Age that froze and melted repeatedly. The last ice sheet carved out the Great Lakes, shaped valleys, deposited moraines, and gouged out the Hudson River Valley. The ice sheet's southern edge included New York City, where the ice was more than 2,000 feet thick.[5] To imagine that depth, think of the Freedom Tower, which is 1,776 feet tall, and the Empire State Building, which is 1,454 feet tall. Both buildings would have been covered by the Laurentide Ice Sheet.[6]

As the ice sheet retreated, it formed a dam, below which was the gigantic Lake Iroquois, three times the size of what would become modern-day Lake Ontario. About 13,000 years ago, the ice dam broke. The waters of Lake Iroquois were unleashed. A massive flood came crashing down through the Hudson Gorge, past Manhattan, Brooklyn, and Staten Island with such force that it smashed through the southern moraine, an earthen dam created by the repeated movement of the glaciers pushing earth and rocks as they advanced south. The force of the flood opened this wall, creating The Narrows, a constricted waterway between Staten Island and

Brooklyn, and forever connecting the Atlantic Ocean to one of the largest natural harbors in the world and the Hudson River. According to Woods Hole Oceanographic Institution geologist Jeff Donnelly, "The water level in Lake Iroquois dropped 120 meters (400 feet), and rocks the size of Volkswagens moved hundreds of miles downstream."[7]

Other massive glacial lakes, Lake Albany and Lake Hudson, emptied out, contributing to the flow of glacial melt that crashed through The Narrows.[8] As a result, the Hudson is not just a river—a body of fresh water that flows from the mountains to the sea. It is also an estuary, an arm of the sea where the ocean meets a river at its lower end and flows north into the river basin. On the incoming tide, the ocean water is pushed up the estuary, and its salt water mixes with the river's fresh water, producing brackish water.

Over tens of millions of years, the ancestral Hudson carved its path from the mountains to the sea, but until the flood, it flowed west of the Palisades, eventually turning east south of Staten Island and flowing into the Atlantic near Sandy Hook.[9] The flooding of Lake Iroquois carved out a new and direct path for the river to meet the sea. And since the last glacial retreat, the Hudson has kept to its course, starting in Lake Tear of the Clouds in the Adirondacks and flowing 315 miles south to the Atlantic Ocean.

The last glacier to move south through the Hudson Valley was the Laurentide Ice Sheet, which deepened the river's channel. As it passed the Hudson Highlands, it sculpted a very deep and narrow gorge between West Point and Constitution Island, past the thirteen-hundred-foot-high peaks of Storm King, Breakneck Ridge, and Bear Mountain. This fjord, known as "World's End," received its name from ship captains who tried to sail through this treacherous chasm where the river runs fast and deep.

The First People

The Lenni-Lenape are the descendants of the first inhabitants along the lower Hudson. In fact, Lenni-Lenape (literally "men of men") is also translated to mean "Original People."[10] They lived along the shores of New York's waterways for more than ten thousand years, starting when the last glacier retreated and the land became habitable. The name Manhattan is derived from the Lenape word Mannahatta, "island of many hills." The Lenape called what we now know as the Hudson the Mahicannituck, "the river that flows two ways."

The people of Mannahatta lived off the land and the water. In the spring, summer, and fall, they traveled the harbor, rivers, and bays in dugout canoes made from felled tulip trees, whose tall, straight trunks could hold more than twenty men and women. In spring, when the rivers filled with migrating fish returning from the ocean to spawn, they fished for American shad, blueback herring, alewife, sturgeon, and striped bass. They ate clams and oysters the size of dinner plates. As summer turned to late fall, they moved camp inland to get away from winter's winds whipping up and down the river. They revered the land, water, plants, and animals they depended upon. Teeming with fish, amphibians, reptiles, birds, and mammals, as well as medicinal and life-sustaining plants, their land was paradise.[11]

Before and After Contact

The trees and flowering plants exuded such sweet smells that European explorers noticed the perfumed air even when they were out at sea nearing the coast and sometimes still quite far away. In the fifteenth century, when Christopher Columbus and his crew approached the Bahamas, Columbus wrote, "There came so fair and sweet a smell of flowers or trees from the land that it was the sweetest thing in the world."[12]

Next was Giovanni da Verrazzano in the sixteenth century, who noticed the trees on the coast "which exhale a very sweet fragrance a great distance."[13] In the seventeenth century, Henry Hudson's mate, Robert Juet, chronicler of Hudson's voyage, remarked on the "very sweet smell" of the land, and Hudson wrote, "The land is the finest for cultivation that I ever in my life set foot upon, and it also abounds in trees of every description."[14]

Adriaen van der Donck, an early Dutch settler and leader in New Netherlands, was called "the Jonkheer"—meaning "young squire." Van der Donck had a sawmill where the Nepperhan River and the Hudson meet. Today the Nepperhan River is known as the Saw Mill River, and Yonkers is named for van der Donck. He spent extensive time with the Lenni-Lenape, getting to know their language and customs, their fishing and hunting techniques, and their reverence for the land and the water.

In his book, *A Description of New Netherland*, published in 1655, van der Donck described how the Lenape fished in the spring and summer and hunted bear, wolves, fishers, otters, and beavers in other seasons. He was enthralled by their knowledge and reverence for the plants and the animals, the land, and the river.

Enamored with this world that was so new to him, he wrote, "The air in New Netherland is as dry, pure, and wholesome as could be desired, and so clear, agreeable, and delicate as would be hard to match anywhere else." Of the Hudson, van der Donck said:

> As to a description of the river, we confess to being unable to do justice to its worth and condition. Besides its considerable trade and commerce, which are not to be despised, the river has fourteen navigable inlets and streams. Some are very big and remain sailable far upstream and may thus be regarded as rivers. This river system and the many rich, fertile fields served by it are well suited for establishing sizable settlements, villages, and towns. The river is spacious and broad, clear and deep, not muddy or weed clogged, and suitable everywhere for mooring and anchoring.[15]

Doing justice to the worth of the river is something thousands of others, before the Dutch arrived and ever since, have tried through words, art, reverence, and respect. Its sparkling beauty, the life it supports, and its length, depth, and breadth have inspired and continue to inspire.

Before European contact, Manhattan's coastline was irregular because it was etched with inlets, canals, streams, bays, creeks, coves, and marshes. Babbling freshwater brooks, like Minetta, flowing through what is now Washington Square Park, emptied into the Hudson. Minetta Brook was fed by springs bubbling up near Sixth Avenue and 17th Street and 21st Street and Fifth Avenue. Paved over in the nineteenth century and built up with apartment houses, hotels, cross streets, and avenues, the brook still flows underground and, until recently, it purportedly still bubbled up a glass tube fountain in the lobby of 2 Fifth Avenue after heavy rains.[16]

One of the deepest natural ponds in lower Manhattan was named the Collect Pond. The Lenape had a large encampment along this five-acre pond where they had a constant source of fresh water and trout. Collect Pond was close to seventy feet deep and was the source of the Lispenard

Creek flowing to the Hudson. According to Eric Sanderson, it was the source of another brook "that took the more direct and steeper route down to the East River, the Old Wreck Brook. Legend has it that on the high tide the Lenape could paddle canoes along the East River, across the Collect, and down to the Hudson shore."[17]

By the early nineteenth century, less than two hundred years after the Dutch and English arrived, the pond had become an open sewer. Slaughterhouses, tanneries, public houses, and nearby shops dumped their waste, including the remains of slaughtered animals, into the pond. In 1811, the city dug a canal to drain the pond, filled it in, and paved it over, naming it Canal Street.[18]

Manhattan, or Mannahatta, the island of many hills, had five hundred hills, eighty-eight miles of streams, three hundred springs, twenty-one ponds, and many ecological communities supporting thousands of species of animals and plants. Traveling up the Hudson before European contact and its destruction of much of the natural world of the island, one would see sandy beaches, salt marshes, red maple swamps, and deep, ancient oak-hickory and tulip tree forests. As late as the 1860s there were still some sandy coves along the Manhattan shore of the Hudson.[19]

There is a painting by Victor Audubon, one of John James Audubon's two talented sons, of the beach in front of the Audubon estate, Minniesland, which stood near the Hudson River at 155th Street. The view is looking north toward Jeffrey's Hook, the rocky outcrop that today is the eastern shore of the George Washington Bridge where the Little Red Lighthouse stands. In the painting, you can see sailboats and men in a rowboat. These men were very likely bringing in American shad and striped bass, the fish that migrated up the Hudson each spring by the millions and fed the Native people and the new immigrants. The artist's father and famous bird and wildlife painter, by then an elderly man, sits on a rock in the sun watching the fishermen bring in their catch. The sun lights up the clouds over the Hudson and patches of the Palisades. A dog stands on the beach looking out toward the river and the breaking waves.

This painting offers a small window into how connected people were to the river. They were able to feed themselves from its bounty. They were able to walk to the river from their homes. When they looked out on the river, they saw natural beauty unmarred by industry. If this painting was created today, the view from 155th Street would be toward Fort Lee, New Jersey, and the George Washington Bridge.

A River of Many Purposes

For thousands of years, up until they were driven from the area in the late seventeenth century, the Lenape bathed and swam in the Hudson. They ate from the Hudson. At most there were ten thousand to fifteen thousand people living in Mannahatta. Within a few hundred years of European contact, there were millions of European immigrants living there. The river became the sewer and dumping grounds of the city as it grew. In his seminal book, *The Hudson River: A Natural and Unnatural History*, Robert Boyle wrote, "The river is all sorts of things. It is a trout stream and estuary, water supply and sewer, ship channel and shad river, playground, and chamber pot."[20]

Boyle was many things, but perhaps most importantly, he was one of the founders of the Hudson River Fishermen's Association (HRFA). Formed in 1966, the group was made up of fishermen and fisherwomen, scientists, and environmentalists. Following Boyle's leadership, the group eventually sued the corporations polluting the river. Not only was the river the main source of their livelihood, but it was a place of beauty and recreation for themselves and their families.

While doing research for a fishing article he was writing for *Sports Illustrated*, Boyle had discovered a couple of old federal laws: the Rivers and Harbors Act of 1888 and the Refuse Act of 1899, both forbidding the pollution of US waters and offering monetary bounties for people who reported any violations. The HRFA subsequently reported Penn Central Railroad, Standard Brands, Ciba-Geigy, American Cyanamid, Anaconda Wire and Copper, General Electric (GE), Con Edison, and many other industries, towns, and counties, including Westchester County. In his book, Boyle writes that Art Glowka of the HRFA came up with a clever way to name names. "He designed pre-paid 'Bag-a-Polluter' postcards. The cards note the New York Harbor Act of 1888 and point out that the person who reports a convicted violator may collect up to $1.25 as a reward." The HRFA printed ten thousand Bag-a-Polluter cards and gave them out to citizens up and down the Hudson Valley.[21]

This bold initiative helped raise awareness about how industry was polluting the rivers, ultimately leading to environmental protection laws enacted in the early 1970s, among them the Clean Water Act of 1972. The HRFA became Riverkeeper, which grew into an umbrella organization of more than three hundred Riverkeeper and Baykeeper organizations around the world that monitor the health of their waterways.

Dirty Business

When I moved to the river in October 1975, raw sewage from every toilet on the West Side of Manhattan, from Greenwich Village to the northern tip of the island, flowed directly into the Hudson. That meant one hundred fifty million gallons every single day. I didn't notice anything until that first summer on the boat. During hot summer days and nights at dead low tide when the river had ebbed out to the sea, the smell was noxious. I would not have dreamed of swimming in the river then.

In addition to sewage, other things were pouring into the Hudson that were affecting the health of the organisms living in it. Between 1947 and 1977, GE dumped up to 1.5 million pounds of polychlorinated biphenyls—PCBs—into the river from their industrial plants along the river at Hudson Falls and Fort Edward, two hundred miles north of New York City. This chemical agent created by Monsanto was used by GE to insulate their products and prevent electrical fires.

By dumping PCBs into the Hudson, GE ended up poisoning the river. The PCBs settled into the riverbed, where they entered the food chain, accumulating in zooplankton, fish, birds, and mammals, including humans who ate the fish. The manufacture of PCBs was banned in 1979 by the Environmental Protection Agency (EPA) when they were found to cause cancer and birth defects.

In 1984, when PCBs were determined to be widespread in the Hudson, the EPA declared two hundred miles of the river, from New York Harbor to Hudson Falls, a Superfund site, designated as such because it contained materials contaminated with hazardous substances. GE was forced to pay for the removal of PCBs and is still, forty years later, being pressured to clean up the mess it made.

The Hudson River Fish Advisory Outreach Project is a multiyear initiative of the New York State Department of Health. It offers the following advice for eating fish caught in the Hudson: "The Sensitive Population (people who may become pregnant (under 50 years old) and children under 15) should not eat any fish or crabs from the Hudson River between the South Glens Falls Dam in Warren County to The Battery in New York City because PCBs may be more harmful to young children and unborn babies."[22]

It wasn't only the PCBs that were killing the river. Waste and pollution from other industries contributed to the loss of native fish and the destruction of a way of life for Hudson River fishermen and fisherwomen and their families.

From 1896 to 1996, a Chevrolet plant sat on ninety acres in North Tarrytown on the eastern shore of the Hudson, about thirty miles north of New York City. It used one million gallons of water per day from the Tarrytown water supply that would flush into the Hudson, carrying with it industrial waste from manufacturing more than sixty cars and trucks per hour at the plant. Lead chromate, a highly toxic pigment used to paint the vehicles, and other chemicals poured into the Hudson every hour of every day. Paint was flushed directly into the river. In 1971, Dominick Pirone, then-director of the HRFA, remarked, "You can tell what color they are painting cars on any given day by what color the river is."[23]

In the mid-1960s, the folk singer Pete Seeger, who lived in Beacon, New York, along the banks of the Hudson, was desperate to do something to protect the river he loved. In 1966, he announced he would "build a boat to save the river," making a replica of the wooden sloops that used to sail the Hudson. This boat, to be named the *Clearwater* to reflect Seeger's vision that someday the river would be healthy again, would bring people to the river so that in sailing the Hudson they would see its majesty and want to protect it.[24]

In 1969, the sloop *Clearwater* was launched, and now, more than fifty years later, hundreds of thousands of adults and over half a million schoolchildren, including my students, have traveled on this beautiful sailing ship, collected and identified fish, crabs, and shrimp, and learned about the history of the Hudson from her crew.[25]

In October 2010, my fifth grade science class participated in A Day in the Life of the Hudson onboard the *Clearwater*. This is an annual citizen science event that monitors the life and health of the river through observations, experiments, and readings. The program takes place every October, rain or shine, from the New York Harbor up to the Troy Dam, covering about 175 miles. Weeks before the event, participating classes receive data collection sheets. Schoolchildren and their teachers gather at established points to collect various data about the river: temperature, dissolved oxygen content, salinity, pH, turbidity, etc. Live specimens are gathered using seine nets from the shore.

Aboard the *Clearwater*, my students monitored fish and invertebrates hoisted onto the sloop by a trawl net, including crabs, shrimp, tunicates, snails, and isopods. The students then identified and measured them before they were returned to the river. The collected data were then submitted to the New York State Department of Conservation's Hudson River Estuary Program and Columbia University's Lamont-Doherty Earth Observatory, the co-organizers of the event.

Figure 26. The New-York Historical Society's *Hudson Rising* exhibit included a photo of Pete Seeger and a model of the *Clearwater* sloop, 2019.

In 2004, the *Clearwater* was named to the National Register of Historic Places because of its importance to the environmental movement.

When the river was polluted with raw sewage and other contaminants, bacteria flourished. Raw sewage contains nutrients that microorganisms feed upon, enabling them to reproduce quickly. Aerobic (oxygen-breathing) bacteria consume dissolved oxygen in the water, depleting this vital gas that fish and other river organisms depend on. The more bacteria in the water, the less oxygen is available for the zooplankton, insects, clams, snails, crabs, shrimp, and 237 fish species that spend all or part of their lives in the Hudson River watershed.

Lacking their usual food sources, menhaden (an important prey fish) numbers plummeted, and the fish that fed upon them had to find other sources of food, depleting the population of striped bass, bluefish, American shad, and other species of herring that lived in the river or migrated to it each spring. Fishes fleeing the Hudson moved to waters that provided nourishment. The outlook for the river was grim.

Passed by Congress in 1972, the Clean Water Act—officially known as the Federal Water Pollution Control Act—provided cities with funding for wastewater treatment plants.[26] In 1985, the North River Sewage Treatment Plant was built in West Harlem along the Hudson between 137th Street and 145th Street. Sewage would be run through a miles-long interceptor sewage line north to south along the West Side to the sewage treatment plant.[27] The plant went online in 1986.[28] For the first time since Europeans came to the island, raw sewage was no longer discharged into the Hudson—except after a hard rain—and bacteria in the river declined quickly. The river started to become habitable again for all life. Seeger's dream was coming true.

In the twenty-first century, there has been notable change. It has been over forty-six years since GE stopped dumping PCBs into the river and more than fifty years since Penn Central Railroad stopped dumping oil into the river at Croton. Additionally, the Anaconda Wire and Cable Company in Hastings-on-Hudson stopped dumping oil, metals, and solvents directly into the river. Along with Seeger and other environmental groups trying to protect the Hudson, we surely have the Hudson River Fishermen's Association, more than any other entity, to thank.

Chapter 4

RIVER LIFE
Inhabitants of the Hudson

I began teaching at The Elisabeth Morrow School in the fall of 1997. As part of the science curriculum, I took my fifth grade students on field trips to the river. For these excursions, Tom Lake and Christopher Letts would meet us near the Englewood Boat Basin, down at the base of the Palisades. Tom, a former president of the Hudson River Fishermen's Association, has been publishing the *Hudson River Almanac* for the New York State Department of Environmental Conservation for many years. Chris is an educator with the Hudson River Foundation. Both know the river intimately.

Tom and Chris would arrive with a large seine net and several five-gallon buckets, while I would bring my own buckets and small dip nets for the children to use. Chris and I would don hip waders that allowed us to walk into the river without getting our legs wet. Chris describes the look and feel of the mucky river bottom as "black mayonnaise," a phrase that captures it perfectly. With each step, I would be extremely aware of the pressure the Hudson's water was exerting on my body as it pushed against the rubber suit and I sank into the muck.

Figure 27. Leslie (*left*) and Chris Letts seining on a Hudson River beach near the Englewood Boat Basin, New Jersey, October 2002.

To use a seine net, one person holds onto the pole at one end of the net, planting it firmly into the shallow riverbed, while another person—always Chris on our trips—walks deeper into the river and makes a wide arc, walking back to the beach. Together, Chris and I would steer the animals toward the beach, and as the net hit the sand, we would close the two ends together to safely trap the animals. Little by little we would open the net, and one by one we would put the animals in our buckets of river water, identifying them as we went: striped bass, white perch, blue crabs, shore shrimp, pipefish, winter flounder, hogchokers, and American eel.

By that time, the North River Sewage Treatment Plant had been operating for eleven years, and it had been twenty-five years since the Clean Water Act was made into law. Gradually, the river was becoming more livable for the animals.

How to Save a Species

Atlantic menhaden, also called mossbunker, swim in large schools near the surface. Swimming in unison, thousands of schooling fish follow a single leader. When they are near the shore, they move close to the surface, where they become easy pickings for some of the many animals that feed on them: humpback whales, dolphins, striped bass, and bluefish, as well as the raptors, such as bald eagles and osprey. Menhaden are sometimes referred to as "the most important fish in the sea," and they are considered a keystone species because they support such a large ecosystem.[1]

In addition to their critical role as prey, menhaden are filter feeders, filtering two million gallons of water per year. They feed by opening their mouths and allowing the organism-rich river water to pass over their gill openings, which filter out phytoplankton and zooplankton. If the river is calm, they open their mouths at the river's surface to filter the plankton floating there.

In the spring, the menhaden migrate from the ocean to feed in the lower Hudson River estuary. Young-of-year menhaden also use the lower Hudson estuary as their nursery, and from summer through autumn, the Tappan Zee—where the river widens to almost three miles across—is teeming with young fish.[2] Their presence helps control the population of phytoplankton, microscopic algae that drift on the river's current. If not contained, the algae reproduce uncontrollably and form harmful algal blooms.

Throughout the seasons, the Hudson River has a murky, greenish-brown color. People who don't understand the cause of this opacity think the river is dirty, but the murkiness in this case indicates a thriving ecosystem. Even in mid-winter there is so much life in the water—both microscopic and macroscopic—because the enormous amount of organic detritus that washes into the Hudson from the large and small rivers and streams throughout New York State becomes food for the river's smallest residents: the zooplankton.

Whenever I'd pluck a clump of seaweed from my boat's lines and look at it under the microscope, I'd find it teeming with fascinating creatures that were feeding, swimming, and thriving on the algae. Minute caprellids, commonly known as skeleton shrimp and looking like microscopic praying mantises, clung to the algae with their tiny rear legs called pereopods, holding their gnathopods (jaw-feet) out, ready to grab food, which can be anything from floating detritus to algae to smaller zooplankton. Their delicate bodies floated back and forth with the movement of the water in the microscope slide, caused by the rocking of my boat.

Caprellids have long, feathery antennae, which can also act as a trap for food floating by. Their bodies are translucent, and as I looked through the microscope, I could see the food moving through their system. I saw an entire world of graceful, competent little creatures going about their very important lives.

Pollution and overfishing caused menhaden populations in the Hudson to decline precipitously for many years. The use of purse seine nets in offshore New York State coastal waters was particularly harmful. As large as six city blocks, these huge industrial nets can catch many thousands of fish in a single haul. The National Oceanic and Atmospheric Administration describes the net as follows: "A purse seine is a large wall of netting deployed around an entire area or school of fish. The seine has floats along the top line with a lead line threaded through rings along the bottom. Once a school of fish is located, a skiff encircles the school with the net. The lead line is then pulled in, 'pursing' the net closed on the bottom, preventing fish from escaping by swimming downward."[3]

In April 2019, then–New York Governor Andrew Cuomo signed a bill prohibiting commercial fishing of menhaden with purse seine nets in New York State waters. At the signing, Cuomo emphasized the importance of biodiversity: "New York has made significant investments to improve our habitat, clean up sources of harmful pollution, and restore a healthy diversity of life to our waters. This critical new law will help us further protect a vital fishery that supports species important to our sportfishing economy, as well as the majestic whales and other marine life that are once again returning to our state's coastal waters."[4]

To further help sustain the population of menhaden in New York City waters, the Atlantic States Marine Fisheries Commission voted on August 5, 2020, to set catch limits so that other animals in the ecosystem would not be hurt by the overfishing of menhaden. This meant using different "ecological reference points," for example, the needs of other important fish such as the striped bass, when setting limits for menhaden. In an article responding to this ruling, The Nature Conservancy stated: "This keystone species is not just important for big fish, dolphins and whales. This little fish is essential for a healthy ocean and a strong coastal economy. From Maine's highly valued lobster fishery, which uses menhaden for bait, to seafood chefs up and down the coast, people and wildlife depend on plentiful menhaden in our seas."[5]

Figure 28. Humpback whale, *Megaptera novaeangliae*, breaching with the Manhattan skyline in the distance. Photo by Artie Raslich / Gotham Whale.

When the menhaden rebounded, other animals in the Hudson flourished, including the largest animal of all—the whale. Whale sightings in New York waters have increased 540 percent since 2009. In 2010, five whales were spotted. In 2018, 272 whales were seen, mostly humpbacks, which feed on menhaden.[6]

Harbor seals also became more common. I still recall the very first time I saw a harbor seal at the marina. It was late on a cold winter night in 2005, and the river was filled with ice. There was a knock on our door, and a neighbor told us that there was a seal sleeping on an ice floe. We threw on our coats and ran down the dock. Sure enough, a beautiful seal—gray with dark spots and huge eyes—was resting on a sheet of floating ice. A small crowd of us gathered in the wind on the rocking dock and watched in awe as this beautiful creature opened its eyes and looked back at us. It was magical. A couple of years later, I started seeing harbor seals haul out on floating docks to sunbathe during the winter and through early spring.

Seeing a seal, for me, was a sacred experience. I had gone fifty years without ever seeing a seal in the wild in New York City and then they

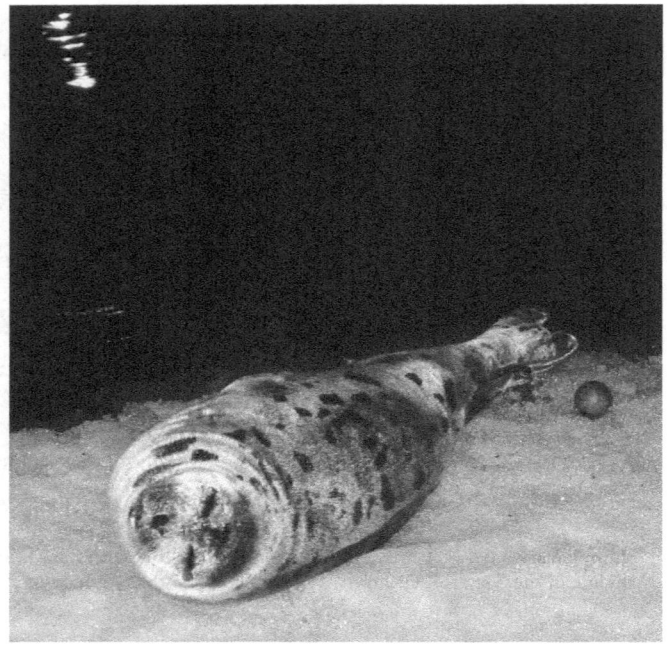

Figure 29. Harbor seal, *Phoca vitulina*, sleeping on an ice floe, February 2005.

Figure 30. Harbor seal, *Phoca vitulina*. Photo by Artie Raslich / Gotham Whale.

were all around me, sleeping on ice floes, sunning themselves on floating docks, and swimming by my boat. They were huge, beautiful creatures with soulful eyes and whiskered, adorable faces that I bonded with immediately. I never wanted them to leave, but after a day of sunbathing, facing east and the sun all morning and then rolling over and facing west all afternoon, they'd dip back into the Hudson and swim away.

Residents of the River

When I was hired to teach middle school science in 1997, I had very little knowledge about the life of the river. Teaching, it is said, is the best way to learn any subject. The happy confluence of events—living on a boat on the Hudson River and teaching fifth graders about the river—helped me immeasurably. Looking, learning, and teaching about the creatures teeming in and around the Hudson, from the microscopic algae and zooplankton to the great American bald eagle and humpback whale, has been one of the great journeys of my life.

Ctenophora: Comb Jellies

In order to closely study the animals of the river, I hung eel traps from a cleat on the dock in front of our boat and baited them with cat food. Every day I'd check the traps, and one summer evening, a slimy substance dripped onto the dock as my husband and I pulled up the trap. He joked, paraphrasing a line from the film *Ghostbusters II*, "We live on a river of slime!"

I put some of the substance into a bucket of river water and poured it into the ten-gallon tank on our kitchen table. Immediately, the "slime" started to swim. We had found comb jellies.

The Hudson is teeming with these creatures, members of the phylum Ctenophores that—despite their name—are not related to jellyfish at all. Ctenophore is from the Greek *ktenos* for comb and *phoros* for bearing, hence a comb-bearing animal. Comb jellies swim through the water by beating their cilia, which are tiny hair-like appendages that form combs. These beautiful marine invertebrates feed on zooplankton.

Most Ctenophora are transparent and bioluminescent: They glow in the dark. The rows of waving combs can bend and refract light, creating gorgeous, shimmering colors. On warm summer nights in July, when I would gently move my hand back and forth in the river, the comb jellies would shimmer purple, blue, and green.

Sygnathus fuscus: Northern Pipefish

The first time I caught a pipefish in my trap, I thought it was just a piece of seaweed hanging from the basket. Northern pipefish, *Sygnathus fuscus*, have thin bodies covered in rings of bony plates and are typically six to eight inches long. Delicate and graceful, they have elegant fan-shaped dorsal and tail fins and long tubular snouts to suck up zooplankton.

Pipefish are close relatives of seahorses, and, like seahorses, the female pipefish deposits her eggs into the male's brood pouch where he fertilizes them. The embryos are implanted next to blood vessels in the brood pouch, which functions as a placenta-like structure where the nutrients are shared between the father and his babies, who are bathed in fluid that is rich in proteins, lipids, and carbohydrates. This is an adaptation because the females produce nutritionally poor eggs.[7]

I kept the pipefish in a ten-gallon tank on our kitchen table, oxygenating the river water with filters, pumps, and aerators. One morning, a few days after I'd caught him, I woke up to see hundreds of what looked like tiny hairs moving around the tank. I scooped out some water and looked at it under the microscope. The "hairs" were baby pipefish.

They looked exactly like the adults but were a fraction of an inch long, with perfectly formed fins, heads, and bodies. I immediately released the father and the babies back into the river. To this day I can still feel the shock of looking through the lens of my microscope and seeing those exquisite baby pipefish and thinking about the miracle of childbearing. I related to that father and his babies. There would be plenty of predators out there in the river, as well as storms, but at least they'd have a chance at life.

Sometimes I brought pipefish into my classroom and let them live in the river tank so my students could study them too. I fed them brine shrimp, and we loved watching them suck up the tiny shrimp with their long tube-like snouts. It was a joy to see how similar pipefish are to seahorses in the ways they swim and feed.

Just like seahorses, pipefish move through the water gracefully, using their small pectoral fins located directly behind their heads, small dorsal fin, and fanlike tail fins to glide. Most of us had only seen seahorses in nature videos, but here were real pipefish living in our classroom.

Trinectes maculatus: Hogchokers

My students and I often caught hogchokers in our seine nets because they are bottom dwellers and were swept up by the net. Hogchokers are one of nine darkly patterned flatfish living in the Hudson River. They got their name from colonial farmers who would feed them to their pigs. If swallowed headfirst, the fish's scales would lie down flat, and they would slide smoothly down the pigs' throats. If they were swallowed tail first, their scales would stick up like teeth on a rasp, choking the hog.

Flatfish hatch from their eggs with an eye on each side of their head. After about a month, the larvae undergo a couple of astounding physical changes to prepare them for their adult stage on the river bottom. Their "top" side becomes heavily patterned so that they blend in with the riverbed, and their "bottom" side stays a pale color. The other change is more dramatic: One eye migrates from one side of their head to join the other eye, so that when they lie on the river bottom, they can see above them with both eyes. Learning about this, my students and I could barely imagine how an eye could move from one side of the head to another. The answer is that while the larval fish is growing, the eye is pushed by the growth of its bones and muscles to the opposite side of its head. In an article with the great title, "How Flounder Wound Up with an Epic Side-Eye," by Carl Zimmer, who covers science for *The New York Times*, Zimmer writes: "Hormones from the thyroid gland trigger larvae to go through this metamorphosis. The hormones switch on genes in the flatfish skull that cause it to change shape, helping to push one eye into a new position. Inside the eye itself, other genes stimulate the growth of neurons so that it can stay connected to the brain as it travels to a new place."[8]

Once when we caught a hogchoker in our seine, Tom Lake and Chris Letts quickly moved it to a tray filled with river sand and water. Right before our eyes, the little fish disappeared as it changed colors to perfectly match the mottled river sand. Masters of disguise, flatfish can expand and contract their chromatophores (cells that contain different pigments), so that they seem to disappear—a lifesaving skill when they feel threatened by a predator.

We brought the hogchoker back to the classroom, and when we put it in our river tank, it quickly swam to the sandy bottom. Over the next several days, as it became more comfortable in its new home, the hogchoker lay flat against the side of the tank, its "blind" side acting like a suction cup, giving us the opportunity to study the side that would normally lie flat on the substrate. Unlike its right side, or "top," which was patterned with black and brown lines and dots over a golden orange body, its underside was pale—it did not need to be camouflaged.

As the hogchoker clung to the glass of our river tank, we could see its left gill flap opening and closing. Fish breathe by taking in water through their mouths. The water then washes over the feathery gills filled with blood vessels that absorb the dissolved oxygen, which is then carried in the bloodstream to every cell of the fish's body. The gill flap, known as the operculum, then opens, releasing carbon dioxide and oxygen-depleted water back out to the sea, river, pond, stream, or, in our case, classroom aquarium.

Anguila rostrata: American Eel

Each fall, Chris would introduce my students to young American eels, so-called glass eels because they are translucent at that stage. He'd often find the glass eels living inside a soda can at the bottom of the river, an easy way to catch them.

The story of the American eel, *Anguila rostrata*, is fascinating. Both American and European eels migrate to the Sargasso Sea, near Bermuda, their likely spawning place. The Sargasso Sea is part of the North Atlantic Ocean, and while a sea is typically identified by the landmass it is near, the Sargasso is the only sea that is not near a major land mass. Instead, it was named for the floating mats of *Sargassum* algae, which spend their entire life floating on the surface, never rooted to the seabed.

The Sargasso is defined by the circulating ocean currents that surround it: to the west, the Gulf Stream; to the north, the North Atlantic Current; to the east, the Canary Current; and to the south, the North Atlantic Equatorial Current. The water is exceptionally blue, with underwater clarity going down more than sixty feet. It is home to many species of animals, as it provides shelter and food for fish, crabs, shrimp, and several types of sea turtles, including leatherbacks, loggerheads, greens, and hawksbills.[9]

When the eels' tiny transparent larvae, leptocephali (slender head), are around a quarter of an inch long, they are ready to leave the sea. They float with the current toward the river mouths along the eastern coast of North America and the western coast of Europe, respectively. The American eel floating to the Hudson is on a journey of almost one thousand miles, and it may take many months, even up to a year, to get there. For European eels, the journey is even longer: a three thousand to six thousand–mile migration.[10]

By the time American eels reach the Hudson, they have metamorphosed into their translucent "glass eel" stage that lasts several months. Their next stage, the "elver" stage, is when they develop a yellow-brown pigment. The small scales of their bodies are covered in a thick layer of mucus that protects them from microorganisms and allows them to travel short distances on wet grass and wet dam faces. On one of our trips to the river at the base of the Palisades, an educator for the Palisades Interstate Park told us that he had seen eels attempting to climb the cliffs.

One year after their elver stage, they enter the yellow eel stage and, amazingly, have yet to become either male or female. They are virtually intersexual, meaning they have no male or female sex chromosomes. When yellow eels reach a length of about a foot they differentiate into male or female. This stage can last ten to forty years.

Once they enter their last stage—the silver stage—their reproductive organs become mature, and they turn a silvery-black color. This is when they are considered adults. During the silver stage, their digestive system begins to degenerate, and they stop feeding. Their pectoral fins enlarge, helping them swim long distances. Their eyes double in size and become sensitive to blue, which enhances their vision in deep ocean water. Females are generally two to three feet long and males are one-and-a-half to two feet long.

The life cycle of the American eel begins and ends in the Sargasso Sea. They start their long journey back from the Hudson to the sea when they enter their silver stage. In the Sargasso, each female will lay up to thirty million eggs, and the males will fertilize them. This is their final act and the culmination of their lives. Incredibly, to date, no one has seen eels spawn or die in the Sargasso, and, in this regard, they continue to remain a mystery.[11]

Callinectes sapidus: Common Blue Crab

As my education about the animals of the river continued, I was surprised to learn that the soft-shelled crabs I loved to eat were in fact the blue crab, *Callinectes sapidus*. The scientific name is poetic, capturing not only the taste but also the grace of this species of swimming crab. The species name, *sapidus*, means savory, and the genus name, *Callinectes*, means beautiful swimmer. And oh, how they can swim.

I would often watch them swimming past our boat, climbing our lines to pick off algae, shrimp, snails, and whatever else they could find to eat. They could also be spotted clinging to the pilings below water level and feasting on the cornucopia of life that colonizes every wooden piling and dock: zooplankton and invertebrates, as well as red algae, brown algae, and green sea lettuce waving back and forth with the current.

Blue crabs are decapods, which means they have ten legs. The front two are large claws used for defense (they can really hurt), predation, and putting food into their mouths. The next three pairs of legs are used to walk. The last two pairs are called swimmerets or swimming legs. These legs are segmented, and each segment is shaped like a small paddle that they wave back and forth like crazy when they swim, almost like they are semaphore flags sending a message.

As crabs swim, they tuck their other eight legs under their body and use only their swimmerets to move. The males, colloquially known as "jim-mys," also use these swimmerets to get the attention of the female crabs, known as "sooks."

As with many other animal species, the male blue crab is brightly colored, and the female is more plain looking. Even so, with blue crabs, the sooks have red claw tips known as chelipeds. The deeper scarlet her "nails" are, the more desirable she is considered by males, perhaps because their claw tips become a deeper red when they are more sexually mature.[12]

Besides noticing red claw tips, one can tell a female from a male by looking at their abdomens, where they carry their flattened tails. The male's tail looks like a rocket ship or the Washington Monument. The female's tail is a rounded dome that looks like the Capitol building.

When the female is ready to mate, she releases pheromones that a male detects in the water. Through the murkiness of the Hudson, he recognizes her red claws and, to get her attention while letting her know he doesn't want to eat her (blue crabs are cannibalistic), he performs his mating dance. Rising high on all six walking legs, making himself as tall as he can, he spreads his two front claws out wide and starts waving his swimmerets at her, signaling his approach. Then he swims to her and embraces her fully with his six walking legs and carries her carefully that way for several days until she molts her hard shell.

Once her shell is soft, they mate. He continues to carry and protect her from other males until her shell hardens and their embrace ends. She then swims off to feed. Up to nine months later, she will use the sperm she has stored to fertilize her millions of eggs, which will be excreted to the outside of her abdomen and form a soft, orange, spongy mass.

At this point, the female is called a "sponge crab." If she mates in the fall, she will winter safely in the muck at the southern end of the estuary and release her fertilized eggs in spring. If she mates in spring, she will spawn in fall. She may release her eggs many times, but her energy is depleted each time she does, which will eventually lead to her death. The lifespan of both males and females is typically not more than three years in the Hudson, the northern part of their range, if they're not first caught for food by humans or predators such as striped bass and bluefish or by winter's cold and ice.[13]

The hatched young, or zoea, will be carried to the ocean where they will grow and molt many times over until they are able to swim back up the Hudson to start the cycle over again. If one were to pull up almost any line dangling in the river during late spring through summer, they would find tiny blue crabs the size of a fingernail with their tiny paddle swimmerets. At that small size, the crabs can't pinch very hard, but they are adorable and grow quickly. I have kept many over the years in my tanks at school and on the boat. I had to release them back to the river once they grew bigger, otherwise they would eat everyone else I had in my tanks.

Morone saxatilis: Striped Bass

Besides the humans who love to eat these beautiful, savory swimmers, blue crabs are constantly pursued by hungry fish, including the fierce predator, the striped bass. After the Chesapeake Bay, the Hudson River is the second-largest East Coast spawning ground for striped bass.

Recreationally, economically, and environmentally important to the life of the Hudson, striped bass spend the first few years of their life in the river. An anadromous fish, they then migrate to the ocean, where they live until they are sexually mature, at which time they migrate back to the Hudson when the water temperature is 58 to 60 degrees Fahrenheit in early spring. The striped bass come back to the same area of the river year after year—the females to release their eggs and the males to fertilize them. They use their keen sense of smell, which some say is stronger than a dog's, to find their spawning grounds. After spawning, they return to the ocean.[14]

Studies of tagged striped bass show that some migrate seasonally up to New England and farther to the Canadian Maritimes, and some migrate as far south as the Carolinas. But regardless of which direction they go, they still migrate back to the Hudson each spring to spawn. Females can release up to three million eggs that are then fertilized by the males who simultaneously release their sperm. Fertilized eggs float in the brackish water of the river for several days before hatching, and the larval fish continue to grow.

I remember one December day, I was feeding dry cat food to the ducks and geese when up swam three large striped bass. Striped bass are voracious and fearless feeders, often charging their prey. Slicing through the water, the bass grabbed the floating food meant for the birds, sometimes even "goosing" the waterfowl until they dropped the food.

Mature striped bass can reach up to ninety-five pounds and grow up to five feet long. The heaviest caught in the river have been around sixty pounds. The seven or eight black, horizontal lines running from gill cover to tail against silvery-white sides gives them their name. My favorite description of striped bass is by naturalist and writer Dave Taft. He wrote, "With the jutting jaw of a mob kingpin and the pinstripes of a Wall Street executive, striped bass swim through the brackish waters of New York Harbor like old-school New Yorkers—as if they own the place."[15]

A graph on the New York State Department of Environmental Conservation's website shows the size of striped bass by age.[16] At six years, they are longer than two feet; at twelve years, they are thirty-nine inches and twenty-four pounds; at fifteen years, they are forty-five inches and thirty-six pounds; and the maximum age, length, and weight is twenty-two years, fifty-nine inches, and ninety-five pounds. These huge animals have been hunted and eaten by people up and down the East Coast for centuries if not millennia.

Because of their economic importance, striped bass generated an environmental movement in the latter half of the twentieth century. It took almost two decades in the courts and the work of multiple groups (including the Hudson River Fishermen's Association, the Scenic Hudson Preservation Conference, Hudson River Sloop Clearwater, and the Natural Resources Defense Council, among them), but Con Edison was ultimately stopped from building the Storm King Power Plant. The establishment of the plant, slated to be built by cutting into the face on one side of Storm King Mountain, would have been a huge visual blight and a massive disruption to the very areas where vast numbers of striped bass come each spring to spawn. In their brilliant *Hudson Rising* exhibit, the New-York Historical Society showed visitors an in-depth look at the decades-long battle to stop Con Edison from building the power plant in the Hudson Highlands. As the exhibit's website states, "Few campaigns to save the environment have had greater impact than the one conducted in the Highlands."[17]

In 1980, the battle was finally won, and the plan for the plant was canceled. Con Edison donated the land to the Palisades Interstate Park Commission and created a twelve-million-dollar endowment. The Hudson River Foundation used money from the settlement to start serious research on the ecology of the river. Perhaps even more important, the success of the conservation groups helped inspire other environmental movements across the country. Most important, the results meant that US citizens had legal standing to sue environmental polluters and degraders in court and that "federal agencies were now required to investigate all relevant facts before granting approvals. The scenic, historic, and recreational character of places could now be protected under the law."[18]

Alosa sapidissima: American Shad

Shad are a type of herring, the largest of the river herrings. The word shad comes from the Old English *sceadd*, meaning "herring." Shad can reach two feet long and six pounds in weight. They are alluring fish with silver bodies that reflect blue and pink, with green upper backs, lavender tails, and large black spots behind the gills, followed by a series of smaller black spots. Their belly scales form a saw-toothed edge. With a forked tail and a streamlined body, they are built for speed.

Like other anadromous fish, American shad spend their adult lives in the ocean, where they feed and gain weight to make the springtime journey up their native rivers to spawn. This migration occurs in mid-April when the water's temperature reaches 50 to 55 degrees Fahrenheit.[19] This same month, one of the first trees to flower in eastern North America is *Amelanchier canadensis*. This native tree has many common names, including shadbush and shadblow, so named because it flowers when American shad (and other migratory species of native fish) ascend the Hudson River to spawn.

For thousands of years, the Lenape awaited the appearance of white flowers in hills and valleys, for the blooms meant the shad were running. Millions of shad would make their way up the Hudson, and the Lenape would head to the river to catch them. Once smoked and preserved, the shad would provide them with protein for the winter. The Lenape would lay the fish on wooden planks of oak or hickory near a roaring open fire and cook them for hours, or they would lay them on racks to dry in the sun, preserving the savory meat for months to come. The Latin name for shad, *Alosa sapidissima*, means "fish most delicious."[20]

Since the mid-nineteenth century, this important fish has been in decline. A variety of factors that include overfishing and the construction of dams that block the shad's attempted migration to their spawning grounds have greatly depleted their numbers. Riverkeeper, along with the New York State Department of Environmental Conservation, has removed more than 1,600 dams in the Hudson Valley—older structures built in the seventeenth, eighteenth, and nineteenth centuries that are no longer in use. The Department of Environmental Conservation is also currently working with Cornell University on a draft recovery plan for Hudson River American shad.[21]

Acipenser oxyrinchus: Atlantic Sturgeon

In the Northeast, we have two native species of sturgeon: the large Atlantic and the smaller shortnose, *Acipenser brevirostrum*. If the blue crab and the striped bass are emblematic of the Hudson, then the Atlantic sturgeon is literally the symbol of the upper Hudson River estuary. As you drive north through the Hudson Valley on roads that cross tributaries feeding into the river, you can see blue and white signs with "watershed" at the top, a blue drawing of the sturgeon on a white background in the middle, and the words "Hudson River Estuary" at the bottom.

Sturgeons arrived on the scene during the Cretaceous period when dinosaurs roamed the earth, and they have been swimming the seas for two hundred million years. They are living fossils. With their pointy snouts (the species name *oxyrinchus* means pointy snout) and huge bodies, Atlantic sturgeon are the largest fish in the river by far and can attain a length of more than fourteen feet and a weight of eight hundred pounds. Prehistoric-looking creatures with cartilaginous skeletons, they have five longitudinal rows of scutes, or external plates, that are bone-like and act as armor. The scutes, which are modified scales, run along their bodies from just below their gills to their tails, protecting these ancient fish.

Four sensitive feelers called barbels emerge from the area between their mouths and the tip of their snouts. Covered in chemoreceptors, these organs are used to taste rather than feel food in the river bottom. Their mouths are on the underside of their heads and are protrusible. Sturgeon can shoot forward or downward, vacuuming up food that is sensed by their barbels, and then spit out any sand, mud, shells, or other debris. They are gentle giants and feed on small fish, crabs, clams, shrimp, and aquatic invertebrates. Hudson River sturgeon can live for sixty years. They are anadromous, spending most of their adult lives in the ocean except for when they come up the Hudson to spawn. After spawning, they return to the sea.[22]

During the mid-1800s, sturgeon were so abundant that they were a staple source of protein for people living along the Hudson. Millions of these fish were caught, and their delicious meat was dubbed "Albany beef." The females were also prized for their eggs, which were used to make caviar. After the Civil War, fishermen started noticing a scarcity of sturgeon. By the 1930s, their numbers were in obvious decline, but they were still being harvested. I remember going to the deli Barney Greengrass on Amsterdam Avenue and 82nd Street with my father, where he'd order smoked sturgeon. It was his favorite fish.

Figure 31. Shortnose sturgeon, *Acipenser brevirostrum*, pulled from the Hudson, February 23, 2006.

Besides overfishing, encounters with boat propellors also lowered the sturgeon numbers in the Hudson. One afternoon in February 2006, I came home from teaching, and Gregory Smith, our then-dockmaster, beckoned me over to a floating dock. There lay a dead, but amazing-looking, short-nose sturgeon he'd pulled from the river. It had a gaping hole in its side, most likely from a boat propeller.

In 1996, New York State banned sturgeon fishing in the Hudson. In 1998, New Jersey and other Atlantic Coast states followed suit, banning the fishing of this ancient animal. In 2012, the sturgeon was listed as an endangered species. For the first time, no sturgeon could be taken out of the water, even to be photographed.[23]

With these protections in place, sturgeon numbers have slowly been increasing, and more females are laying eggs in the Hudson River estu-ary. These fish are slow to mature and might not lay eggs until their twentieth year, but the young live in the river for up to six years before they move south into the Atlantic. Finally, they have a chance to rebound and roam the seas again as they've been doing for hundreds of millions of years.

Aurelia aurita: Moon Jelly

Translucent jellyfish known as moon jellies are commonly seen in the Hudson, floating north or south with the current. Looking into their bells, you can see the four horseshoe-shaped gonads, where the males produce sperm, and the females produce eggs. The four tentacles, also known as oral arms, contain nematocysts—stinging cells—that the jellyfish use to paralyze their prey. Then the arms transfer the prey to their mouth. (They cannot sting humans because our skin is too tough.) Their prey are small zooplankton, mollusks, and crustaceans. You might find one washed up on a beach, a round hardened disk of its pellucid moonlike bell.[24]

Cyanea capillata: Lion's Mane Jellyfish

Each summer, like clockwork, as the air and water temperature heated up, lion's mane jellyfish would pass our boat. Looking out my window and into the river I could see the pulsing of their red bells and their long trailing tentacles as they floated by, carried by the current. Typically, one or two would pass a couple of times a day, but in July 2008, during the swim portion of the New York City triathlon, when 3,000 swimmers jumped into the Hudson at 98th Street and swam to the 79th Street Boat Basin, scores of lion's manes were present in the river. One swimmer who was stung, a twenty-four-year-old woman, told *The New York Times*, "I thought the water was radioactive or something."[25]

Like moon jellies, lion's mane jellyfish stun their prey with nemato-cysts, injecting neurotoxins into the animals that brush against the jel-lyfish's tentacles.[26] Once the prey is immobilized, oral arms move it to the lion's mane's mouth.

The jellyfish can't control where their tentacles drift. The attack is trig-gered upon contact, whether the tentacle contacts a moon jelly (a common prey) or a human swimmer, and the nematocysts of the lion's mane can penetrate human skin. I was stung one summer while visiting friends in Martha's Vineyard. Swimming in a beautiful bay, I suddenly noticed I was surrounded by a swarm of very small lion's mane jellyfish. I made for shore, but I must have brushed against their tentacles. The intense burning pain was immediate.

Phalacrocorax auritus: Double-Crested Cormorants

When I moved aboard the *Mandala* in 1975, my sweet first boat at the marina, the only birds I saw on the river other than gulls were large black diving birds called double-crested cormorants (double crested for the ear tufts they bear during mating season). You've probably seen them, sitting atop pilings or jetties, holding their wings out to dry. They look like pterodactyls—flying reptiles that lived among the dinosaurs—and evolutionarily, cormorants are an ancient species of bird.

Double-crested cormorants are stunningly beautiful creatures, and although their body and tail feathers are black, their wing feathers are bronze etched in black. They have orange skin around their face and

Figure 32. Double-crested cormorant, *Phalacrocorax auritus*, holding its wings out to dry. Copyright © Beth Bergman.

throat and the most gorgeous emerald green–aquamarine eyes. When they open their bills during breeding season, you can see the bright electric blue lining of their mouths. Their young are more tan than black, with pale necks and throats.

Cormorants cannot only fly but they can also swim underwater while hunting for prey, holding their breath for up to a minute and reaching depths of twenty-five feet. Living on my houseboat, I watched many of these mighty birds wrestle three-foot-long eels. It was a shocking scene. The birds would swallow the live eels whole, and even as they moved down the birds' gullets, the eels kept thrashing.

Cormorants spend so much time diving for fish that their feathers become saturated with water. It was initially believed that they had no uropygial gland—the preen gland that produces oil. If you watch almost any bird, you will see them rub their bill and head in a spot on their rump, just above the tail. This is where the gland secretes oil that they then cover their feathers with as they preen every barb—the individual fiber that makes up a feather. The oil makes their feathers waterproof and helps keep them in good shape for flying, staying warm in winter, and keeping cool in summer. Now it is known that the cormorant has a working uropygial gland just like any other water bird, but cormorants spend so much time completely submerged chasing after fish that their feathers become saturated and heavy, which actually helps them stay under water.[27]

When my students—both children and adults—studied birds, I would always have them do feather experiments with water. They would fill pipettes with water and carefully squeeze droplets onto the large turkey feathers that I would collect from the campus of The Elisabeth Morrow School, where small groups of wild turkeys foraged throughout the year. Each drop of water would land on the feather and stay there, like a round sparkling gem.

Drop after drop would move toward each other as if they were magnetized, and if the students tipped the feather, the large drops would roll right off—like water off a duck's back. This is because water and oil don't mix. Anyone who's waxed a car and then watched raindrops bead up on the hood has seen this phenomenon.

Eventually, if enough water was added, the feather would become soaked, and the oil would stop working as a protective shield. That is the same thing that happens with cormorants—as they dive, their feathers become saturated. To become more hydrodynamic, they swim with their wings held against their body. Their webbed feet are far back on their body, and they use them like synchronized flippers, propelling themselves forward at close to six miles per hour.

Cormorants are colonial nesters.[28] They are social animals, and they nest in groups, all the better to protect each other. (Because of this communal habit, their accumulated poop or "guano" tends to kill the trees they nest in.) I got to see this nesting behavior firsthand when I was writing my book *Field Guide to the Neighborhood Birds of New York City*.

In 2013, Don Riepe, then-manager of Jamaica Bay Wildlife Refuge, took me and the science staff of New York City Audubon cruising on his boat to a colonial nesting island in Jamaica Bay. The very first thing we saw as we approached the island was a tree full of nesting cormorants. The scene reminded me of a Dr. Seuss drawing: The birds sat high in their nests with sticks jutting out in every direction, and there was a family of cormorants in every nest on every branch. Adding to the comical effect was the fact that adult cormorants stand over their babies like awkward umbrellas to shade their young—all of whom looked an awful lot like little dinosaurs.[29]

Falco peregrinus: Peregrine Falcon

I love the Hall of North American Birds at the American Museum of Natural History. The museum has been a part of my life for as long as I can remember. When I was a child, my family would visit my grandparents on West 73rd Street every Sunday. While the adults would sit, eat, and visit with each other, my brother and I would walk up Columbus Avenue and enter the museum on West 77th Street, between Columbus and Central Park West. At that time, David and I would mostly just play hide-and-seek among the totem poles in one of the oldest wings of the museum. It wasn't until I was in my late thirties that I started really studying the birds in the museum.

The Hall of North American Birds boasts numerous dioramas that depict habitats and include taxidermied birds and their food—the plants that produce the berries, flowers, and seeds they consume and for raptors, their animal prey. Frank Chapman, an ornithologist who was the curator of birds at the museum during the early 1900s, helped create the hall with birds from every habitat on the continent. Chapman is also known as the "Father of the Audubon Christmas Bird Count," the longest-running citizen science endeavor in the world.[30]

In my favorite diorama, a peregrine falcon adult is carrying a dead pigeon to its nest on a rocky ledge of the Palisades with the Hudson River below.[31] The peregrine falcon is the fastest animal on earth. With a plummeting flight called a stoop, they can dive-bomb their prey, typically a smaller bird, at over two hundred miles per hour, knocking it out of the sky. The peregrine falcon lives on every continent of the world except Antarctica. Its Latin species name, *peregrinus*, means "wandering falcon."[32]

Peregrines prefer to nest on stony outcrops overlooking their hunting grounds. The architecture and infrastructure of New York City has millions of stony ledges, providing these predators ample opportunities to create their nests, or scrapes. Unlike the nests of other birds, a scrape is not made of nesting material. Rather, it is simply made from a depression in the gravel, leaves, soil, or anything that sits on top of the stone. This small dip helps ensure that their beautifully colored eggs—mottled red, purple, or rich brown—don't roll out.

Peregrine pairs stay together for life and reuse their scrapes each year. In June 2022, a pair of peregrines built their nest in the belfry of the St. Paul and St. Andrew United Methodist Church on the corner of West 86th Street and West End Avenue. Birders and photographers from all over the city watched the falcon family throughout the summer. There are established peregrine nests on the George Washington Bridge, the Broadway Bridge in Inwood, the Gill Hodges Bridge in Queens, and Riverside Church on Riverside Drive and 122nd Street, and many more nests have been discovered on New York City sites over the years. There are more peregrine falcons in New York City than in any other urban area in the world.

This level of abundance is particularly gratifying, given that these magnificent animals were almost driven to extinction in the 1950s and 1960s. At that time, the insecticide DDT was used on farms, in gardens, and in backyards. The DDT ran off into waterways and was absorbed by food webs. The birds that ate the insects, berries, fish, and crabs absorbed the DDT into their systems. Smaller birds, such as robins and warblers, died

Figure 33. Peregrine falcon, *Falco peregrinus*, sitting in a tree on the Palisades at Greenbrook Nature Preserve, Alpine, New Jersey. Photo by Gloria Nelson.

from the toxicity. Larger birds—raptors like bald eagles, peregrine falcons, and osprey—survived but started laying eggs with very thin shells. The shells were so thin that when a parent sat on the eggs to incubate, the eggs would break from the bird's weight. These raptor species then started to die out as well.[33]

Scientist Rachel Carson fought against the pesticide industry and wrote her seminal book *Silent Spring* in 1962, raising awareness of the peril our birds faced.[34] By 1972, DDT was banned, and bird populations started to recuperate.

Haliaeetus leucocephalus: Bald Eagle

From the time I started identifying and learning about the birds of New York City until our move to a high-rise building in Riverdale in 2021, we lived at sea level. Our home in Riverdale is maybe half a mile from the Hudson, and we live on the twenty-third floor. High above the trees, we can now see the raptors that glide and soar over the river and the neighborhood: bald eagles, ospreys, peregrine falcons, kestrels, red-tailed hawks, and northern harriers.

Figure 34. Bald eagle, *Haliaeetus leucocephalus*, soaring over the Hudson.
Photo by Gloria Nelson.

We see the fish eaters: bald eagles throughout the winter and osprey in spring and summer. When I first read John Kieran's account of seeing bald eagles on the ice floes in the Hudson River, I was jealous.[35] I'd never seen a bald eagle in New York City.

The first time I saw a bald eagle in the wild I was in my mid-forties, and we were swimming in the Schoharie Creek near our cabin in the Catskills, when one flew right by me. Another time, we heard about a bald eagle nest in Prattsville, near the Schoharie Reservoir, and we drove to the site to look up at a huge nest in a conifer tree. Bald eagles build their nests in the tallest trees they can find, and the nests are impressively large. They can be up to nine feet across, twelve feet deep, and weigh more than one thousand pounds.

Bald eagles can live up to thirty years in the wild. Juveniles are uniformly dark brown with a gray bill. They don't gain their bright yellow bills, white heads, and white tail feathers until they are about five years old. They reach a massive wingspan of up to six feet.[36]

Bald eagles were driven nearly to extinction through hunting, trapping, and pesticide poisoning. They were saved by the banning of DDT and the Endangered Species Act. What a joy it is to be able to watch these amazing raptors from my terrace as they soar over the Hudson River.

Pandion haliaetus: Osprey

The osprey, also known as the sea hawk, migrates to our area in the spring and stays through early fall. Their genus name comes from Pandion, a mythical king of Athens whose daughters were turned into birds. Their species name, *haliaetus*, means "sea eagle." The common name osprey derives from the Latin *avis praedae* meaning "bird of prey."

Osprey, like bald eagles, are native to North America, but unlike the eagles, the osprey migrate south in the winter to find open, unfrozen water so that they can fish. Ospreys are large raptors, dark brown above and white below. Their head is capped by a white crest with a brown cheek patch from their beak across their eye to the back of their head. Viewed from below, they have arched white wings with dark wrist patches.

Ospreys perch on dead tree branches near water and fly out over the water where they hover and dive, often completely submerging themselves. They rise with fish in their talons and, in midair, arrange the fish so that it is oriented headfirst. This reduces wind resistance as they fly to a perch or nest to feed themselves or a female and chicks. Ospreys can fly thirty to forty miles per hour but reach eighty miles per hour when diving for fish.

These large birds build enormous nests that can reach twelve feet deep and six feet in diameter. They are constructed on top of trees or on human-made platforms, always next to water. The building itself is a collaborative effort. The male carries the sticks to the female, and she arranges them. Once the nest is built, she lays two to four mottled cream-and-pink eggs speckled with cinnamon brown. The male feeds her as she incubates the eggs. When the eggs hatch, he feeds the entire family for as long as two months, carrying three to six fish a day to the nest. An osprey will stay with its mate for its entire breeding season or, in some cases, for life.[37]

Figure 35. Osprey, *Pandion haliaetus*, with a striped mullet in its talons.
Photo by Rolando Yera.

Nycticorax nycticorax: Black-Crowned Night Heron

In all the decades I lived on the Hudson, the only heron that regularly visited the marina to fish was the black-crowned night heron. Year after year, a heron would show up in spring, and I would see it standing on the dock, on the boat lines, or even on electrical and phone cables suspended above the docks. It stood with its head and long spear-like bill pointed toward the river, watching and waiting for fish to appear before diving in, catching a fish, and flying back to the dock or wires to feed.

Whereas the bald eagle, osprey, and peregrine falcon are diurnal and feed during the day, night herons are nocturnal. They sleep in trees during the day and fish at night. As dusk fell throughout each summer evening, we would hear their call, "Quark!" as they flew over the marina. (A common name for this heron is the quark bird.)

They are a common sight in New York City wetlands throughout the warm months, and they are beautiful creatures. Two feet tall with a four-foot wingspan, they have blue-gray backs, gray wings, black crowns, and ruby red eyes. Adults are pure white on their undersides, though juveniles are brown streaked with white. When night herons are breeding, both the males and females grow two long white breeding plumes.[38] They nest in large nesting colonies in New York Harbor on Hoffman Island, in the Jamaica Bay Wildlife Refuge, and on South Brother Island in the Bronx.

Gulls

The three gulls we would most commonly see were the ring-billed gull, the great black-backed gull, and the herring gull.

The most abundant species of the three in our region is the ring-billed gull (*Larus delawarensis*). In winter, we would see them flying overhead in huge numbers or assembling on the breakwater dock at the western end of the marina. This long dock was built to break up fast-moving wakes from passing boats and was always empty during winter. The large flocks of wintering ring-billed gulls would congregate there. During the coldest

Figure 36. Ring-billed gull, *Larus delawarensis*, looking into the houseboat on a snowy day.

parts of winter, when the river was frozen or choked with ice, the hungry gulls would call and beg for food. I would throw dry pellets of dog food or cat food onto the ice. The gulls would land and slide toward the food, sometimes skating on the ice with their large, webbed feet. Other times they would catch the food in midair. This was thrilling for me—feeding them like this as they'd hover and swerve, calling and calling. With the cold wind in my face and hair, I felt a sense of freedom and lightness just watching them float on the air high above me.

Aptly named, the ring-billed gulls have black rings around their yellow bills. During summer breeding, their heads are pure white. Non-breeding adults have speckled tan and gray streaking on their heads in winter. Their bodies and tails are white, and their black wing tips are spotted with white. Juveniles are speckled brown and white. In spring, ring-billed gulls move north to lay their eggs and raise their young, leaving a few juveniles behind by the river.[39]

The great black-backed gull (*Larus marinus*) is almost as large as a bald eagle—up to three feet tall with a wingspan of almost six feet. They are scavengers, stealing fish and crabs from other birds, and they are also fierce predators. Although commonly seen along the Hudson, in spring they join nesting colonies on islands in New York Harbor, the East River, Jamaica Bay, and the Long Island Sound, where they gather seaweed, sticks, grasses, and feathers and build nests on the beach near beachgrass. Adults have a large, bright red spot near the tip of their yellow lower bills, which their chicks tap when they are hungry.[40]

Smaller than the great black-backed gull and larger than the ring-billed gull, the adult herring gull (*Larus smithsonianus*) is white with a gray back and wings, black wing tips with white spots, and pink legs. Like the black-backed gull, the herring gulls have a large, red circle on their lower bills.[41]

During the icy and cold winter of 1994, I found an injured young herring gull thrashing in the river near E dock. It was stuck between large chunks of floating ice. Jim and I were able to put a blanket around it and put it in a large cat carrier. We found a vet listed in the Lower East Side who worked with birds, and we brought the injured gull to his office. This was before the Wild Bird Fund opened on the Upper West Side—the first licensed wildlife hospital in Manhattan—or we would have taken the injured gull there. We drove downtown and carried the gull into the examination room. As soon as the vet pulled the gull out, it grabbed his thumb with its large, sharp bill and bit down. That poor man just wrapped his bloody finger up and continued with the examination. The gull had a broken wing. The vet said he'd set the wing and thought it would be able to fly once the bones healed, and if that happened, he'd release it near the Hudson.

Herring gulls spend time on the river during winter but will often build nests directly on the tops of buildings during breeding season in spring and early summer. One building that serves as the Manhattan breeding ground of a colony of herring gulls is the Javits Center. It is a huge glass convention center along the Hudson that spans four square blocks. The center created a seven-acre green roof filled with sedum plants that the herring gulls love to nest on. During the summer of 2022, there were 150 herring gull nests on the roof of the center.[42]

One More Very Special Species

The Lenape people lived in this area for more than ten thousand years. They named the village they lived in Shorakapok, meaning "edge of the river." (That area is now known as Inwood Hill Park in northern Manhattan.) Going back to 1609, before the arrival of Europeans, more than half of the world's oysters lived in the lower Hudson estuary. During the spring, summer, and fall, the Lenape lived off the animals of the river and ate so many oysters that wherever they camped they left huge piles of oyster shells, known as oyster middens. Middens have been found in Washington Heights at West 175th Street along the Hudson and in Inwood at Dyckman Street, Isham Street, and Inwood Hill Park, as well as up and down the Hudson Valley in Ossining and Croton Point. The largest and oldest Atlantic Coast shell midden dates back to 6950 BC and can be found in Dobbs Ferry, New York.[43]

These middens contained sturgeon scutes; turtle, deer, dog, snake, bear, and turkey bones; stone axes; arrowheads; pottery; stone mortars and pestles; hair ornaments made of fish bones; tomahawks; and bone needles. The biggest middens could stand as tall as an adult and would have the largest oyster shells at the bottom. It takes years for an oyster to grow, and the largest ones from any one area were eaten first.[44]

When the Europeans arrived in the area and first tasted the American oyster, *Crassostrea virginica*, they were delighted by the enormous size, mouthwatering taste, and seemingly endless supply. Jasper Danckaerts, who arrived in New Amsterdam in the mid-seventeenth century, tasted oysters roasted by a friend living in Gouanes (now Gowanus, Brooklyn), and wrote back home to Holland:

> We proceeded on to Gouanes, a place so called, we arrived in the evening at one of the best friends of Gerrit, named Symon. He was very glad to see us and so was his wife. He took us into the house and entertained us exceedingly well. We found a good fire, half-way up the chimney, of clear oak and hickorys, which they made not the least scruple of burning profusely. We let it penetrate us thoroughly. There had been already thrown upon it, to be roasted, a pail-full of Gouanes oysters, which are the best in the country. They are fully as good as those of England, and better than those we ate at Falmouth. I had to try some of them raw. They are large and full, some of them not less than a foot long, and they grow sometimes, ten, twelve and sixteen together and are then like a piece of rock. Others are young and small. In consequence of the great quantities of them, everybody keeps the shells for the purpose of burning them into lime.[45]

When Henry Hudson first sailed up what is now the Hudson River, there were roughly 350 square miles of oyster beds between the harbor and Haverstraw Bay, the large bay that flows beneath the Tappan Zee Bridge and connects Rockland County on the western shore of the Hudson with Westchester County on the river's eastern shore. The Dutch names for what we call Ellis Island and Liberty Island, where the Statue of Liberty now stands, were Little Oyster Island and Great Oyster Island. These islands, revered by the millions of immigrants who entered the United States on their shores over the last 150 years, were surrounded by oyster beds. Until humans made the water uninhabitable for these animals, the oysters were so plentiful that people could simply walk out at low tide and harvest them from their beds.

But as each new group of immigrants arrived, they too discovered the oysters. Unlike the Lenape, numbering in the thousands and living lightly upon the land, these new residents of New York arrived in great numbers, eating billions of oysters. They poured sewage and other pollutants into the rivers and ultimately annihilated perhaps the world's greatest population of oysters.

As another keystone species—an essential part of the Hudson River estuary's ecosystem—oysters give and give through their extraordinary ability to filter water. As they filter, they extract all kinds of pollution, including nitrogen, which comes from decomposing animals and plants and lately from fertilizer runoff. Too much nitrogen in the water can lead to marine "dead zones," an area where oxygen levels are so low that aquatic life cannot survive. Oysters use the nitrogen for food and to build their shells. A single oyster can filter up to fifty gallons of brackish water every day. When billions of these incredible animals were feeding twenty-four hours a day, seven days a week, the waterways were pristine and healthy.

In addition, oyster reefs provide habitats for a multitude of fish and aquatic invertebrates. They also act as wave attenuators, reducing both the height and the energy of waves during storms and protecting the coastline from flooding and erosion.[46]

As early as 1891, William K. Brooks, a scientist at Johns Hopkins University, wrote, "In the oyster we have an animal, most nutritious and palatable, especially adapted for living in the soft mud of bays and estuaries, and for gathering up the microscopic inhabitants and turning them into food for man."[47]

Brooks warned of the calamity oysters were facing in the Chesapeake Bay as they were being harvested by the millions each year and shipped across the country. This could have been a warning for the people of Manhattan, but it was not heeded. By the 1900s, oysters were virtually nonexistent in New York Harbor. Peter Malinowski, cofounder of the Billion Oyster Project, offered an apt description of the area: "Imagine New York Harbor as a 200,000-acre forest that's had all its trees removed."[48] It took until the twenty-first century, more than four hundred years after the arrival of Hudson, for New Yorkers to finally realize the important role of oysters and what their loss has meant for the entire lower Hudson River ecosystem.

River Rescuers

Over the years, I've learned that there are many groups of creative people who have devoted their lives to protecting the Hudson, and many of them have interconnections. In 2005, while on a Circle Line ferry ride hosted by the American Museum of Natural History, I ran into Lisa Breslov, my former boss from when I taught after-school science classes to high school students at the museum. Lisa introduced me to her friend Murray Fisher, founder of the Urban Assembly New York Harbor School and cofounder, along with Peter Malinowski, of the Billion Oyster Project.

The New York Harbor School was housed in the Bushwick Campus High School when it opened its doors in 2003, and it is now thriving in its current location on Governors Island, where it moved in 2010. The high school recruits students from the five boroughs and offers a curriculum that teaches environmental leadership, particularly in the context of maritime careers.

Their website further elaborates: "Our students learn to build and operate boats; spawn and harvest millions of oysters; design submersible, remotely operated vehicles; conduct real-life research; and dive underwater. [Our] students go on trips, tour colleges, hear and learn from experts in science and industry and participate in the school's on-going oyster restoration research program through The Billion Oyster Project."[49]

Peter Malinowsky grew up on an oyster farm on Fishers Island in the Long Island Sound. The farm is owned and operated by his parents, whom he credits for his vision of environmental stewardship. Peter cofounded the Billion Oyster Project with Murray in 2014 with the goal of restoring the health of New York Harbor by reestablishing its oyster reefs. Originally a project of the New York Harbor School, the program grew and evolved into a citywide initiative, now boasting the participation of one hundred schools, dozens of restaurants, and thousands of community volunteers.

Ira Gershenhorn is one of the local volunteers working with the Billion Oyster Project to help meet its restoration goals. Once a week during the spring, summer, and early autumn, Ira goes down to the *Baylander* at 125th Street on the Hudson. The *Baylander* is a decommissioned US Navy helicopter landing ship. It was billed as "the world's smallest aircraft carrier" and served as a landing site for helicopter pilots in the US military during the Vietnam War and for years afterward. Now it is both a popular restaurant and bar and an Oyster Research Station site for the Billion Oyster Project. It is one of more than two hundred sites throughout the city that have live oysters submerged in cages in the city's waterways, all monitored and maintained by students, teachers, and community scientists.[50]

Ira monitors baskets of oysters hanging from ropes off the cleats of the ship. When he pulls the baskets up, he measures each oyster. In a logbook, he records the date, the temperatures of the water and the air, and the size of the oyster shells. He also emails these data to scientists who are analyzing the best way to restore oyster reefs to the waterways around New York City.

I joined Ira in the summer of 2020 to help collect data. I felt rewarded each time he pulled up a basket and we put any fish, crabs, and invertebrates into a basin filled with river water. It was an immense delight to see my old river friends: a young toadfish, baby blue crabs, isopods, shrimp, and—most delightful of all—young oysters that were thriving.

Restaurants and fisheries from all over New York donate oyster shells to the Billion Oyster Project. The shells are put in baskets and lowered into the lower Hudson River estuary, from the New York Harbor to the Tappan Zee. The shells are important because oyster larvae look for hard surfaces to glue themselves to before they grow their own shells.

Oyster reproduction is a fascinating process. Males and females look the same, but when the temperature of the water is at least 68 degrees Fahrenheit, the female oyster releases her ten million eggs, and the male oyster releases his sperm. The adult oysters must be near each other for fertilization to take place. The fertilized eggs quickly become tiny larvae that swim for several weeks.

When they are ready to live a life on the riverbed, they sink down and use their "foot" to explore the muddy bottom, searching for an oyster shell to settle onto. When they find their new home, they absorb their foot and glue themselves to the oyster's hard shell or any available hard surface. At this point they are called "spat." It takes two to three years for the little oyster to become fully grown and ready to reproduce.[51]

To date, as of February 2025, the Billion Oyster Project's website shows that it has collected close to three million pounds of recycled shells from restaurants, restored 150 million living oysters, and installed seventeen oyster reefs across New York Harbor. We are a long way from one billion oysters, but this trajectory is encouraging. It is my dear wish that as my granddaughter Aya grows up along the shores of the Hudson, she will know a river where this keystone species is once again thriving.

Chapter 5

WEATHERING

Storms and Other Threats to the
79th Street Boat Basin

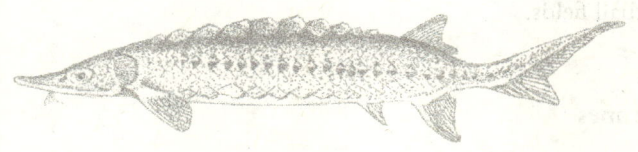

In late September 1985, Hurricane Gloria was hyped as a storm that would wreak havoc on the city. The headline of *The New York Times* warned: "Major Hurricane Threatens Middle of East Coast."[1] Meteorologists indulged in alarmist language. Watching television days before the storm, I remember one TV weatherman saying something like New York City was staring down the barrel of a gun.

To prevent the predicted shattering of glass, apartment-dwellers taped giant X's on their windows. Boat owners like my family were frightened we would lose our homes and our unique way of life, and some made plans to evacuate. (Mandatory evacuations weren't enacted until decades later, but by then Jim and I had moved to land.) I took Jonah and our dogs Spot and Maya up to my grandmother's apartment on West 73rd Street. Jim stayed on the boat ready to evacuate if need be.

Our neighbors Raquel and Werner Buhrer left the marina and motored their houseboat upriver to Kingston, New York, where they thought they'd be safe. However, hurricane-force winds almost sank their boat, and they had to be rescued.

New York City got lucky. On September 27, Gloria made landfall on Fire Island. Many towns in Long Island were flooded, and Connecticut named it "the storm of the century," but Manhattan itself was spared. The wind clocked in at fifty-five miles per hour at the marina. Gloria was nothing more than a windy rainstorm on the Hudson at West 79th Street. Jonah and I kissed my grandmother goodbye and walked our dogs down the hill and back home to our boat.

Autumn and winter are the typical seasons for devastating storms on the river. These seasons were nerve-racking times for us, as our little floating community was completely exposed to the winds, ice, and flooding that accompanied hurricanes and nor'easters. Not to mention ice floes the size of football fields.

Hurricanes

High winds caused by storms can increase the surge of water during high tide. On October 29, 2012, Hurricane Sandy made landfall during high tide and broke the record for storm surge height in New York City. Water rose nine feet higher than normal, and flooding was extensive. The rivers surrounding Manhattan Island jumped their banks and flowed into subway stations and car tunnels, drowning low-lying areas like the Lower East Side and the shores of Staten Island. In Breezy Point, Queens, a small community at the tip of the Rockaway Peninsula, over one hundred homes caught fire when seawater contacted electrical wires.

Mayor Michael Bloomberg ordered a mandatory evacuation of Zone A, including Manhattan's southern tip—Coney Island and Red Hook—the entirety of the Rockaway Peninsula, most of Staten Island, City Island, and the Throggs Neck area in the Bronx. The New York Aquarium in Coney Island was so badly flooded that when people came in to check on the animals, they found Mitik, a baby walrus who'd arrived only weeks before after being orphaned in Alaska, swimming around in fifteen feet of seawater in the basement.[2] The south shore of Long Island and the Rockaways were flooded, and people were trapped in their homes for days. The New York Stock Exchange closed for the first time since the attacks of 9/11.

At the time Sandy hit, we had been living on land for a year and a half. Our boat, the *Sanibel*, a forty-three-foot Marine Trader, was in dry dock in a marina on City Island that had been evacuated. Worried about the condition of our boat, Jim started looking at pictures of the marina online. He finally found a photo taken two days after the hurricane: in it, a small sailboat, the *Ciao*, sat on the cement, listing to the right with a broken keel. To the left, somehow still upright and fine, was the beautiful *Sanibel*. She had made it through, but a chapter was closing for us.

In June 2014, we sold the *Sanibel* to a man with a seasonal permit for the Boat Basin. Seasonal permits lasted from April until October and then the boat had to be moved to a different location. He used the boat as a pied-à-terre in spring, summer, and autumn. Then, like other seasonal residents, he decamped for the winter. This had the effect of emptying out the marina, leaving only a handful of year-round boats and making life there even more vulnerable and isolated, especially during the most dangerous of seasons.

Winter Woes

The properties of water cause ice to form on its surface. As the water surface cools, the movement of water molecules slows down. Below 32 degrees Fahrenheit, the molecules start to assume fixed positions. They stay connected by their hydrogen bonds but spread out, becoming less dense than liquid water and rise to the top. This is why ice floats.

The Hudson flowing by New York City is an estuary, an arm of the sea on the incoming tide. It is a brackish mixture of salt water pouring in from the Atlantic Ocean and fresh water pouring in from the rivers and streams of the Adirondack and Catskill Mountains, as well as the Hudson Valley. At high tide, as ocean water pushes up into the river basin starting in New York Harbor, salt molecules bond with water molecules. The temperature needed for salt water to freeze is 28 degrees, four degrees lower than for fresh water.

The more salt there is in water, the lower the freezing point. This is why the Hudson estuary that flows past the city becomes choked with ice when the ice floes that form north of the city start to flow south through Haverstraw Bay, beneath the bridges, past Washington Heights, Harlem, and the Upper West Side, eventually reaching the harbor. Then, at the incoming tide, those same massive ice floes begin moving north at a grindingly slow but powerful pace. Eventually they crash into the Boat Basin, where there is very little ice protection.

Moving ice is as dangerous a force as fire, flood, or high winds. The ice, sometimes almost two feet thick in a very cold winter, can cause tremendous damage to the boats, pilings, and docks of a marina, giving those of us who lived on the river some of our most terrifying and beautiful images and memories.

In the dead of winter, I could always hear the heavy throb of tugboat engines, even miles away, as they pushed barges laden with heating oil upriver. Sometimes the ice was so thick that Coast Guard cutters would work day and night keeping a path open so the barges could deliver their millions of barrels of fuel to heat homes throughout the Northeast and Midwest. They also needed to keep the channels open for the ferry boats that carried eight million commuters from Staten Island, New Jersey, Brooklyn, and Queens to Manhattan and back.

There is a history of ice floes on the Hudson stretching back millennia. In his book, *A Description of New Netherland*, Adriaen van der Donck wrote:

> In March 1647, when a strong ice flow from above had made the river fresh as far as the sea- at normal tide, fresh water comes down to twenty or twenty-four miles from the sea- two fairly big whales swam more than forty miles up the river. One turned back and became stranded, later freeing itself at a spot eleven or twelve miles from the sea where four others were stranded in the same year.[3]

The blizzard of March 1888, in which my great-grandfather lost his hearing as he made his way home to Avenue A and East 10th Street, was a week of terrible ice on the Hudson. In a *New York Times* story on March 14, the headline reported, "Uncertain Ferry Traffic. Boats Irregular in Trips and Delayed by Huge Ice Fields." The article stated:

> Floating ice in immense fields and floes interfered very seriously yesterday with the running of the ferryboats. The terrific tempest of Monday and

Monday night had driven all the loose ice in the Hudson down toward the Bay in the constantly enlarging fields, which the fierce snow and cold bound together in solid masses. These caught the flood tide early in the morning and swerved off into the East River and massed in the Bay and Hudson River in fields that spread from shore to shore. Against this mass that was almost solid ice and the gale that was still blowing, the ferryboats made but irregular progress.[4]

During my own decades on the river, there were multiple winters when ice devastated sections of the marina. The winter of 1977–78 brought brutal cold to the mid-Atlantic states. Ponds and lakes froze so quickly that the feet of swans, geese, and ducks became stuck. The Hudson froze solid, and our seventy-four-year-old neighbor Paul Jordan, his much younger girlfriend, Barbara, our neighbor Ed Bacon, and a neighbor's daughter all went out and skated on the ice.

As the river began to thaw, massive sheets of ice started to move and cut down the pilings of the Basin as easily as if they were matchsticks. Years later, Ed recalled the event in his *Boat Basin BULLetin* newsletter: "There is nothing like the sound of wood being smashed and splintered

Figure 37. (*from left to right*) Seventy-four-year-old Paul Jordan ice-skating with Ed Bacon, Barbara, and a neighbor's child off D dock, 1978.

by ice at three in the morning to get your attention."[5] His own boat at the end of D dock was saved by neighbors who helped him move it to a slip further east—away from the moving ice floes and closer to land where the current wasn't as strong.

The next winter was equally bad. On a frigid night in February 1979, the ice was so thick that it once again mowed down the wooden pilings. Chains were used to attach the narrow finger docks between boats to the pilings that were still standing. My husband left the boat to take Spot and Maya out to the park for their final late-night walk.

Both dogs were rescues. Jim and his first wife found Spot tied to a tree in Riverside Park and took him home. I found Maya or, more accurately, Maya found me just a month after I moved onto the *Mandala*. I had been walking through the park toward a yoga class when a gangly German shepherd/husky mix jumped up on me, circling my legs and wagging her tail. She was young and very skinny.

I never made it to the yoga class. I put my scarf around her neck and walked her to a vet up the street. He said, "Congratulations! You found yourself a beautiful dog." I took Maya back to the marina with me. When we reached the floating dock, she dropped down on the wooden planks and belly-crawled along the dock until we got to my boat.

On that freezing February night in 1979, Jim came back just minutes after he left. His beard and mustache were covered in ice, and his eyes were wide behind foggy glasses as he entered the boat. He told me that Spot had disappeared.

This was terrible news. If Spot had fallen into the river, he would have a slim chance of surviving. The air temperature was in the single digits, the water temperature was in the thirties, and the ice was on the move. I don't remember exactly how I rounded up neighbors to help us search for him. You can communicate an emergency on a boat by blasting your horn (most boats in the Boat Basin had a boat horn or at least an air horn) five times—the navigational signal for danger. I'm not sure if I did that or just called neighbors, but soon enough there were six big men inside our tiny boat, and the hunt for Spot began.

They were out on the dock for a long time but—miraculously—they eventually came in with a very wet and very cold dog. It was not easy to see a black dog at night in a dark river, but it was sound that saved Spot. Our dear friend and neighbor Ray Stephens heard jingling metal. When he aimed his flashlight toward the sound, he saw Spot in the river, clinging to the dock and shaking so violently that his collar tags banged together.

A secondary winter hazard were the howling winds that drove river water over the docks, making them icy and treacherous—fine locations for slips and falls. In the winter, we were all especially lucky to have Ray as our neighbor.

We had all moved to the marina in 1975: Ray in June, Jim and Leah in August, and me in October. Jim was my neighbor on the east side, and Ray was my neighbor on the west side. A skinny little Irish American with a great sense of humor and a silver tongue, Ray quickly became my best friend at the marina. The first week I lived there, I heard a shout and ran out of my boat. There was Ray pulling my dripping wet cat, Nessim, out of the river. I adored him from that moment on.

Ray had been a medic during the Vietnam War. When he returned to New York he became a physician's assistant at Metropolitan Hospital on East 96th Street and First Avenue, where he worked with orthopedic surgeons. His skills made him the go-to person at the marina for injuries. As the Queen of Sprained Ankles, I accumulated quite the assortment of bandages and braces over the years—all given to me by Ray.

It was so cold and windy the winter that Ray lived on the western end of E dock that the entire surface of his dock froze. On some mornings, he had to crawl on his hands and knees down the dock to get to work. Another time, he dreamed he was waiting for the 79th Street crosstown bus. In the dream, he thought it was strange that the sidewalk was moving up and down. He slowly opened his eyes and realized he was looking at the lights of New Jersey. He had sleepwalked and was standing in his pajamas on the narrow catwalk of his boat, holding his briefcase in the middle of the night and waiting for the 79th Street crosstown bus that would never come.

About a year after we moved from the Boat Basin to Washington Heights, Ray was diagnosed with brain cancer. He died in 2013. It was a terrible loss for his family who adored him and for all of us whose lives he enriched.

Along with the other harsh challenges of winter, we worried about access to fresh water for drinking, bathing, and cooking. Extremely cold temperatures for weeks on end could freeze up the entire freshwater line for the marina, and the only remedy was to keep the water running continuously from December through March. The line was a long series of connected hoses that ran on each of the five docks. If it froze, people from each dock would disassemble the hoses and take a length into their boats to warm it up. Once the hoses were thawed, we would reconnect them, and the water would run again. The system was fragile. Any kink could freeze the entire length of hoses and cut off our source of fresh water.

During one particularly brutal winter in the mid-'90s, we had a new dockmaster who turned off the water because he didn't want to see it "wasted." This, of course, froze the entire line and cut off water to more than one hundred families. He said, "I'll guess you'll have to wait until a thaw." We took it upon ourselves to thaw the frozen hoses and get the water running again.

In mid-February 1994, the ice came down from the north and choked the river shore to shore. Jim was once again out late walking our dog Molly (Spot and Maya had passed away years before) when he heard a loud crack. He thought it was the line holding the camel—a wooden dock that barricaded and protected the south side of the marina from ice flowing north on the incoming tide. He came back to the boat and told me we had to get our son, our cats, and our most precious possessions. He insisted we had to move everything and everyone to the car, which was safely parked in the marina garage under the West 79th Street Rotunda.

Skeptical, I went outside. What I saw was shocking. The ice had pushed several boats up onto our dock and E dock (the southern-most docks), and enormous ice floes were moving north toward the marina. Our neighbor Delta Willis's houseboat, the *Delta Queen*, had been pushed by the ice into a piling. Our friends Werner and Raquel's houseboat at the western end of D dock was also pushed up onto the dock. I blasted our horn five times and went door to door. People came out with boat hooks, broomsticks, axes, and other tools to chop the ice.

Four men, including our intrepid dockworker Troy Porter, by then in his late sixties, jumped on the ice floe behind the Buhrer's houseboat. They chopped and hacked at the ice to break it up. Eventually the tide ebbed, and the ice moved south, away from the marina.

That summer we had a dock party and celebrated our survival of a treacherous winter on the river. From Raquel and Werner's railing, we hung photos of icebergs, boats that had been pushed onto docks, and

Figure 38. Ice damage to docks, February 1994, looking south between D and E docks.

Figure 39. Troy Porter (*far left*), Didier Murat (*sitting on ice*), Doron Katzman (*with shovel*), and Werner Buhrer (*far right*) break up the iceberg between D and E docks that pushed Werner and Raquel's boat, the *Raquelita*, up on D dock, February 13, 1994.

Figure 40. Neighbors on the dock celebrate surviving the river of ice of 1994.

people standing on the ice breaking it up. We toasted the river and each other, happy to still be living on the water, safe from winter's fury, and enjoying days of warmth, camaraderie, and gorgeous sunsets.

Boats are not insulated, and although we covered our windows with shrink-wrap plastic every winter, cold easily penetrated the boat. Over thirty-six winters, Jim and I tried every kind of heater available: kerosene, propane, diesel, wood, coal, pellet, and electric. My favorite heater was a cast-iron, wood-and-coal-burning Jøtul stove from Norway. It was a thing of beauty, with an enameled burgundy cast-iron exterior and a pony design on the front. It kept us warm even when the outside temperature was below zero. We also burned coal—filthy, but it produced a tremendous amount of heat.

It wasn't easy to find coal in New York City. We found a place in the Bronx where they'd weigh our old Volvo station wagon as we drove in, then weigh it again on our way out when it was filled with one hundred–pound bags of coal, charging us by the ton. When that place closed, we hired a coal truck to come to the marina. The truck had sliding doors on its side that opened to coal bins beneath. We'd hold our one hundred–pound

Figure 41. The *Tranquility* houseboat glows on a cold winter's night, February 1996.

burlap bags under the bins and fill them up. When that service ended, we drove to 126th Street in Harlem. After that, to Closter, New Jersey. Soon coal was no longer available, and we bought a stove that burned wooden pellets. When we got our cruiser, the *Sanibel*, our last boat at the marina, Jim installed a diesel heater.

Nor'easters

The worst storms during the thirty-six years that we lived on the river were nor'easters, so named for the direction the wind comes off the Atlantic. Nor'easters affect the eastern coastal regions from the mid-Atlantic to Canada and are very much like cyclones. They typically form during fall through late winter/early spring, and their winds can reach hurricane force of sustained seventy-five miles per hour. If it is cold enough, blizzards form, bringing high winds and huge amounts of snow. Extremely high tides are also common.

In mid-December 1992, as Jonah and I walked up the hill to school—he to middle school IS 44 on West 77th Street and me to the Calhoun

School on West 74th Street—the wind was so strong that when Jonah leaned back into it, it held him up. He laughed and laughed, but I thought, This is not normal.

Nonetheless, I started the day with my four-year-old students. One of them came late. Her father said that the Hudson River had flooded onto the Henry Hudson Parkway at 102nd Street—the parkway's lowest point along the river. I couldn't remember this ever happening before. I immediately called Jim, who was at his lab at Brooklyn College, and said, "Better come home."

I left school, and as I ran down to the river, I could see a pair of huge white swans flying back and forth over the marina through the rain and wind. I had never seen swans at the Boat Basin until that day.

According to NYCdata, a website run by the Baruch College Weissman Center for International Business:

A "Nor'easter" hit New York City (NYC) on December 11, 1992 and caused pandemonium in all of the five boroughs. It brought with it wind speeds of 70 mph and devastating storm surges. What made the Nor'easter so destructive was the fact that it was slow moving. It created high tides with dangerous consistency and caused many low-lying areas to flood. Con Edison experienced flooding in Manhattan, resulting in a disruption of the flow of electricity to NYC subway lines. As a result, the MTA had to shut down for more than 3 hours. LaGuardia airport also had canceled flights because of flooding. Sections of FDR Drive were underwater in Manhattan, and many drivers, trapped in their vehicles, had to be rescued by scuba divers. Heavy snowfall was recorded in some regions of New York. However, many areas saw little to no snow during the storm. Coastal regions especially prone to flooding were hardest hit, with boardwalks and boats washing away into the ocean. The City set up many shelters for evacuees in schools and in fire houses.[6]

The rain came down hard and fast, and the river kept rising. For the first time, I felt irresponsible for raising my family on a boat. I felt like the stupid little pig who built her house of straw. I called the mother of one of Jonah's friends and asked her to pick him up from school and take him home with them to their apartment building on West End Avenue to wait out the storm. At least he would be safe in a building made of solid brick.

Figure 42. Nor'easter, December 1992, floating home destroyed.

That night, Jim and I never went to sleep. We put our valuables, cats, and dog in our car in the Boat Basin garage and returned to the boat. We stayed in our clothes and kept our boots on. Through the night, we watched the river rise until there was only an inch left of piling above the water. At that point, the tide finally started to go out. Our boat and the marina were saved. Had the river risen above the pilings, the boats tied to them would have been pulled below the surface. As it was, the northernmost dock, A dock, was lifted off its pilings and crashed into several boats, sinking them. The storm raged for three days.

Sinking

For most of our years at the Boat Basin, we and the majority of our neighbors lived on boats that did not run. As the saying went at the marina, we were floaters not boaters. It wasn't until we bought the *Sanibel*, a fully running and, to me, luxurious boat, that we nearly sank. The *Sanibel* had two bedrooms, two bathrooms, an eat-in kitchen, and two decks.

At five thirty one morning in late October 2008, Jim woke me abruptly and said, "We're sinking!" I couldn't find my glasses or even my phone, so I ran down D dock and up to the end of C dock to Ed Bacon's boat. Ed was an experienced sailor. He had moved to the marina in 1970, five years before me. He was an IBM systems engineer and, at that time, newly divorced.

My first week at the marina I knocked on his window with a question. He told me to come back later and said that he was "working on [his] head." I thought, He's in therapy. In fact, he was working on his toilet. A ship's toilet was named the "head" by sailors because it was at the head or the bow of the sailing ship, just above the water line, where wave action could wash it out.

Ed was there in every emergency at the marina, so on that chilly October morning, I stood outside his beautiful sailboat, the *Prelude*, calling for help. Ed grabbed a set of wooden plugs and ran to our boat. He quickly

Figure 43. Gracie Mansion book launch of Leslie's first book, *Field Guide to the Natural World of New York City*, November 7, 2007.

found the leak: A thru-hull fitting had popped out overnight during a very low tide, allowing river water to flood our bilge.

I couldn't help but think about Mayor Michael Bloomberg's prescient question to me the night of the release party for my first book, *Field Guide to the Natural World of New York City*. The event was held at Gracie Mansion on November 7, 2007, almost one year before our sinking. Bloomberg had written the foreword for my book, and he introduced me, reading from his notes. When he got to the part about where I lived, he stopped reading and looked at me with raised eyebrows. With surprise in his voice he asked, "Really? You live on a boat?!"

And then, the kiss of death: "Did it ever sink?"

After our brush with sinking, Ed wrote about it in his *Boat Basin BULLetin* and offered some very useful advice. I was mortified but, of course, he was right.

Near sinking

Before dawn on October 29, a Basin vessel began to sink. The owner heard the water rushing in, the leak (the boat speed transducer had popped out of its thru hull) was found, a tapered wood plug was inserted, about a foot of water in the bilge was pumped overboard and a diver later plugged the opening. Some issues surfaced:

- You can't give the five blasts danger signal if your ship's horn and hand-held horn don't work. Check them out.
- You can't call your neighbors and the dockmaster's office unless you have the contacts information handy. No time to wait until your computer boots up.
- If you're trying to get your sleeping neighbor's attention, don't just yell from the dock. Bang on the hull. Guaranteed to wake the soundest sleeper.
- If you hear the danger signal and you have a portable crash pump, be sure it's stored in a handy place so that you can quickly grab it and take it along with you.
- Make a sketch of all your thru hulls, both below the waterline and near the waterline.
- Ensure that the Basin's large pumps are brought to the scene. Your onboard pumps may not be able to keep up with the water flow from a 1–2" open thru hull two feet below the surface.[7]

9/11

On the morning of September 11, 2001, I drove my usual passengers to school: three of my fifth grade students who lived near me in Manhattan. As I made the loop from the Henry Hudson Parkway west onto the George Washington Bridge, I remarked to the kids sitting in the back seat, "I think that's the bluest sky I've ever seen."

In New York City, we make fun of days like that, saying, "This is a top ten day!" because we rarely get more than ten perfect weather days in a year. But it really was a top ten day. No wind, mild temperatures, no humidity, a clarity in the air, and the bluest of blue skies.

My first teaching period was free that morning. As I walked toward the office, I ran into my friend, Lisa Nicolau, our writing teacher and a wonderful poet and writer herself. She was pale and shaken. She said she had heard on the radio on her way to school that a plane had crashed into the World Trade Center. I went back to my classroom and turned on the radio.

At first, the newscasters reported that it was an accident. The buildings were still standing, but there was a burning, gaping hole near the eightieth floor in the North Tower. Hundreds had been killed, and many more were trapped in the floors above. Less than twenty minutes later, the second plane struck the South Tower. At that point the head of our school, David Lowry, and our principal, Germaine DiPaolo, told the homeroom teachers to keep the children in their rooms. Some of the teachers, including me, gathered in the library with our librarian, Eleanor Schuster, to watch the news on television.

By 10 a.m. the South Tower collapsed. At 10:30 the North Tower did too. I remember Dr. Lowry saying, "That's it, bring all the children into the gymkhana," a building that served as a gymnasium and our auditorium. We all filed in, and Germaine asked the children if any of their parents worked in Manhattan. If my memory is correct, six little hands went up. Germaine asked them to come to her office with her. The rest of us tried to go on with our day.

I went back to my classroom and my students showed up, among them a boy named Emilio. Emilio was an intelligent and caring kid. He asked me to tell him what was going on. When I said I wasn't sure, he begged me, saying, "Something is going on, and we need to know what it is."

So I told him. I remember he was helping me as I cleaned the cage for Luna, our royal python, a gentle and calm snake. He was holding her, and he looked at me and said, "You know what today's date is, right? 9–1–1."

Parents began picking up their children immediately. No one could enter Manhattan by any of the tunnels or bridges. The parents of the twins I had driven to school picked up their children and kept heading west to a house in New Jersey. I don't remember if the third student, Kai, went with them or if he went home with a friend, but I do know that his mother, Janet Cogsville, worked across the street from the World Trade Center and had watched it crumble to the ground. She walked home to 145th Street from downtown, at least six miles, her eyes swollen and almost closed shut from the particles and dust that filled the air.

Our dockmaster at the time, Gregory Smith, built a shower on the fly that he hung from the C dock gate for the thousands and thousands of people marching north from downtown. The day turned hot and dry, and people were thirsty and covered in dust. Many stopped at that shower in Riverside Park on that awful trek home.

A parent of three of my students, Christine Evron, was in the city that day and made several trips with her station wagon, ferrying people from downtown to the bridge before heading back downtown to find more people who lived in New Jersey and needed a ride to the bridge. The walk from downtown to the George Washington Bridge is about ten miles. So many walked those miles, covered in dust, traumatized, and hurting.

As for me, I could not get home. All cell phones were down. Finally, I heard from our son. At that time, he worked in a stained glass studio in the Bronx. There were no subways or trains running, so he had no way of getting home until one of his colleagues loaned him a bicycle. He rode to a subway station in the Bronx and got there just as the subways started working again. My husband managed to eventually come home from Brooklyn College.

I tried to drive home, but when I got to the bridge all traffic into the city was blocked. Masses of people were waiting on the New Jersey side for their families and friends who were walking over the bridge. I went back to my classroom, and my colleague Carolyn Milne, her husband George, and their son-in-law Lee Pillsbury showed up and took me to dinner.

Afterward, we got on their boat at the Englewood Boat Basin, and they tried to take me home on the river. When we were just below the George Washington Bridge, we were stopped by a phalanx of small Coast Guard boats with flashing blue lights. No one was allowed into Manhattan. I explained that I needed to get home to my family, but they gave us a firm no. We went back to Englewood, where Carolyn and George kindly let me sleep over at their house, though sleep did not come. The next morning, the bridge was finally opened, and I was able to go home.

Immediately after the fall of the towers, for the first time in over a century, the only way people in lower Manhattan could get off the island was by foot or on a boat. Within a half hour of the plane hitting the South Tower, all public transportation was shut down. New York City's Emergency Operations Center, located inside the World Trade Center, was destroyed, buried in the rubble. There were no cars, taxis, buses, or subways available. By 11 a.m. everyone in the area below Canal Street was ordered to evacuate.

It took the quick thinking of Lt. Michael Day, a Coast Guard officer who witnessed the World Trade Center attack, to reach out to boat owners, captains, and deckhands to help with the rescue. "All available boats," Day called into his radio. "This is United States Coast Guard. Anyone wanting to help with the evacuation of Lower Manhattan, report to Governors Island."[8]

Boats on the Hudson raced toward Manhattan to help people escape. An armada of more than 150 boats, including large ones like the Staten Island Ferry and boats from Circle Line Sightseeing Cruises, came together to rescue the throngs of people who were escaping from their offices, apartments, schools, stores, streets, playgrounds, and houses of worship. People were jumping into the river to escape the acrid smoke and blasts of debris from the falling towers. This extraordinary maritime mission rescued almost half a million people that day. It was the largest boat lift in US history. It was like an American version of the Dunkirk evacuation.

I asked Ed—who had been chartering his boat, the *Prelude*, for others to use for many years—what he remembered about 9/11. He recalled,

> We were on the wave wall. We saw on a morning show that a light plane had hit the north tower. We went above and others from inside the Basin arrived

since they could not see the [World Trade Center buildings] from their slip. Through my binoculars, I saw the second plane hit the south tower. Delta Willis immediately said "Osama Bin Laden" since she knew of the [1998] Nairobi US embassy bombing [conducted by al Qaeda]. Tom Purrington, an ex-pilot, said "That was no light plane."

Ed immediately got to work chartering boats for news organizations but soon had to stop.

Our best client on *Prelude* was Dave Westin, [then the] ABC News president. [ABC News] called asking for multiple boats to take them downriver. We placed Charlie Gibson on *Argo* [a historic ferryboat owned and captained by Chris Williamson] and Diane Sawyer was coming to board *Prelude* when we heard the river was closed. We asked to start ferrying people from the Basin but were refused. . . . No boats from the Basin participated in the evacuation. We could have helped so many people looking for a way to get to New Jersey with the [bridge] and all the tunnels closed.

For what seemed like weeks, our deck was covered in dust and particles. I swept it off every day. Cavalcades of sanitation trucks went up and down the Henry Hudson Parkway and the West Side Highway to carry away the massive amounts of debris from the fallen towers. Sleep was difficult, and the stories were terrible. Missing person flyers were everywhere. People held out hope until they couldn't anymore. Thousands had died. The city and the world mourned.

For the next eight years, life was relatively peaceful on the river. We resumed our day-to-day lives with work, school, and seasons passing, and then something amazing happened on the Hudson. Something that made us all smile then and still makes me smile to this day.

During the first two weeks of January 2009, the river was free of ice. On the morning of January 15, a Thursday, I fed the ducks and Canada geese, including Hurtwing, before I left for school. I finished teaching that day around 2:30 and headed home with my dog Sadie in the car. The boat was a mess, and I decided to straighten up and vacuum.

I liked to listen to WNYC on the radio at home. I was vacuuming the carpet in our tiny living salon when I heard the radio announcer say that a plane had crash-landed in the Hudson River near 59th Street. *Wait— what?!* I turned the vacuum off and ran to the upstairs deck looking up and down the river. I saw police boats, fireboats, and Coast Guard vessels, all racing south on the Hudson. I went back downstairs and turned on the TV.

US Airways Flight 1549 had taken off from LaGuardia Airport around 3:25 p.m. At some point, the newscaster said, the plane was struck by a flock of Canada geese. *Oh my God. Were they my geese?* I looked out on the river and saw the usual suspects, mallard ducks and Canada geese.

The landing of Captain Chesley "Sully" Sullenberger's flight 1549 is called the "Miracle on the Hudson" because not one soul was lost. Sully ditched the plane just opposite Port Imperial in Weehawken, where some of the NY Waterway ferries were docked. These ferries, along with boats from the New York Fire Department (NYFD), Coast Guard, New York Police Department (NYPD), and others rescued every passenger, many of whom were waist-deep in 36 degree water.

It was also a miracle because the river had not yet started to freeze. There was ice north of the city on the Hudson but not in the river off Manhattan. On the day of the crash, the air temperature barely made it to 20 degrees Fahrenheit, one of the coldest days so far that winter. The water must have been unbearably cold. One person swam from the floating plane to Manhattan and another to a waiting ferry. Many were treated for hypothermia, but because there was no ice and because of the skills of Sully, his copilot, the crew, and the quick action of the rescuers, no one died.[9]

It was awhile before I learned that the geese that struck the plane were flying south. Feathers were removed from the sunken plane and sent to the bird lab at the Smithsonian's National Museum of Natural History. Carla Dove, head of the Feather Identification Lab at the museum, was interviewed by *Smithsonian* magazine to discuss their findings. The birds that struck the plane were not year-round residents but birds migrating late in the year, escaping an increasingly cold and snowy winter north of New York City. They were looking for land and open water that had not yet been covered in snow and ice. They crossed the path of the plane at 3,200 feet, somewhere above the Bronx Zoo.

Dove shared feathers from the crash with Pete Marra, an ornithologist at the Smithsonian's Migratory Bird Center at the National Zoo. Marra had been using a technique known as stable isotope analysis to discover what birds eat and therefore where they live. The isotope deuterium varies by latitude, and Marra discovered that the geese that were sucked into the engines of flight 1549 were male and female Canada geese in one engine and a female in another engine. Marra referred to analysis of feathers from bird strikes as a different kind of black box recorder, providing the exact species that caused the disaster and whether they were in their breeding grounds or feeding grounds or migrating between them. Or if they were residential geese—my great fear.

Data showed that these ill-fated geese were originally from the Labrador region of northeastern Canada. Plane engines today are designed to be able to withstand a bird strike from birds that are four pounds or under. Migratory Canada geese typically weigh eight pounds, residential geese even more.[10]

Two days after the plane crashed into the Hudson, there was a thaw with temperatures rising to the thirties. The ice north of the city started to break up and move south. Less than a week after the Miracle on the Hudson, moving sheets of ice floated on the Hudson's surface. If that bird strike had happened a week later, the plane would have had to ditch into an ice-choked river, causing a much more devastating impact on a hard, icy surface.

Resilience in the Boat Basin

The city has tried to keep people from living on their boats for decades. But despite the long history of attempts to remove the year-round houseboat community, the city has largely been unsuccessful. One of the gravest threats we faced was following a fire in 1980.

One early morning in late October 1980, as we left the marina to go to work, we were greeted at the gates by the NYPD. The officers were handing out notices that we would have to remove our boats by November 30. The New York City Parks Department, then led by Commissioner Gordon Davis, decided to shut down the marina based on concerns from the NYFD's head, Augustus Beekman, that the marina was a fire hazard.[11]

In late September 1980, a transient wooden boat, docked alongside a newly constructed breakwater dock on the outside of the marina, had burst into flame. The boat's owner had docked the boat, locked it up, and went up to Broadway for dinner. Meanwhile, the boat leaked gasoline, which was ignited by an electrical short on the vessel. The entire wooden breakwater, coated with creosote to prevent rot, also burst into flame. We watched the fire consume the boat and then jump to the breakwater dock that ran south from C dock.

We grabbed our two-month-old son and ran out to the park. Firemen showed up quickly and put out the fire, but the incident sparked a potential end to our way of life. My husband was then-president of our boat owners' group, the Hudson Harbor Preservation Association. He reached out to the venerable New York Law School, established in the 1890s by disgruntled Columbia Law School professors, and asked for recommendations of someone who was good in community law. He was given the name of Lonn Berney, a ferocious and precocious young attorney who had his own radio show and liked to stand up for the little guy.

Our neighbor, Joe Fitzpatrick, head of the Office of Public Information in City Hall, was an ex-newspaper man who got advanced warning from an old friend on what Commissioner Davis was about to do. Joe helped arrange media exposure while gathering support from the city council, including influential members Ruth Messinger, Henry Stern, and Fred Samuel. Lonn had us protest outside of the courthouse on the day that we sued the city to prevent them from closing the place we called home.

Judge Kenneth Shorter of the New York State Supreme Court presided. I remember sitting in the courtroom holding Jonah in my arms as Lonn presented our case. Weeks later we were overjoyed when we received the judge's verdict:

> Over the years, a custom has evolved for many boat owners to live year round on the boats with their families and close relatives. There is now a recognized community of some 130 persons in residence at the Marina.
>
> That the "boat people" are integrated into the larger West Side community is attested to not only by the fact of eight families having minors attending local schools, but also by the supportive testimony of City Council members Fred Samuel, Ruth Messinger, and Henry Stern.[12]

Judge Shorter added stipulations that the Parks Department had to fix any fire hazards at the marina. A new exit gate was built by the city between D and E docks. Dock boxes filled with fire hoses were installed

Figure 44. A party with neighbors and Molly the dog, celebrating Leslie's fiftieth birthday, August 20, 1995.

Figure 45. Dear friends (*from left to right*) Werner and Raquel Buhrer, Ray Stephens, Trudy Smoke, Alan Robbins, and Jonah Nishiura (*seated*), 1990.

on each dock. Ed and others organized fire drills. In his closing remarks, Judge Shorter wrote, " 'New York, New York, it's a helluva town.' So sings the poet. So say the people. Mere volume in area, in numbers, and in activity are not together enough to command that prestige. Inextricably woven in the fabric of New York are intrinsic special facets which magnetize the attention and magnify the appreciation. Among them, the West Side boat community." [13]

And with those words, we were free to live on our boats, in our floating small town, our magical village.

Chapter 6

GOODBYES

I started writing this chapter in March of 2020, safely ensconced in my two-bedroom apartment in Washington Heights. The storms we had faced during our almost four decades of living on the Hudson felt like nothing compared to the storm we were facing then—a pandemic, with New York City as the US epicenter.

Through a serious of unfortunate events, Jim and I both caught COVID-19 in the first wave. On March 14, we'd gone to our local Costco on East 116th Street off the FDR Drive, where we had to wait in line to be allowed into the store. Once in, we raced through, getting all our food. Then, while Jim went to the car, I went to pay for our parking in the garage. As I was putting my credit card back in my wallet, I tripped over something on the ground. Falling, I hit my head on a parked car, then bounced backward, landing hard on my knees. My glasses and one of my hearing aids went flying, and I crumpled onto the floor of the garage.

Jim was a few rows away loading the car, oblivious to what had happened. Luckily, two men nearby saw the whole thing and came running.

They tried to get me up, but I couldn't move because of the intense pain. Eventually I managed to call Jim on my cell phone. He brought the car around, and one of the men helped me hobble into the passenger seat. Jim drove us straight to the emergency room, though we both knew, with the pandemic raging, that it was a terrible time to be in a hospital.

At the New York-Presbyterian Allen Hospital on West 218th Street, I sat in a wheelchair for nine hours, surrounded by very sick people. Some of them were trying to lay down in upright chairs, unable to hold their heads up. All of the bays in the ER were taken. There were no masks, no gloves. It seemed impossible that we wouldn't get sick. They released me after x-raying my knees and giving me a CAT scan. I had no concussion, but I did have multiple fractures in my right kneecap. I was sent home with an immobilizer—a soft cast that kept my entire right leg straight.

One week later, Jim came down with the virus, and three days after that I started having symptoms. I lost my senses of smell and taste and had an intermittent sore throat, up and down fevers, headaches, body aches, cough, nausea, and vomiting. All the symptoms. It took at least six months for the fatigue to lift. Jim had been diagnosed with Parkinson's disease two years before we caught COVID-19, and all his symptoms got worse. His speech, his gait, his balance. All around us people were dying. We lost several dear neighbors. Somehow, we survived.

Twilight of the Liveaboards

The storms were terrible on the river, but no one died from them. Boats and docks were repaired. Life went on. People in the Boat Basin were hardy. You had to be. Just to get on and off your boat, you'd have to climb steps and then hop over a narrow watery chasm onto the catwalk of your boat. And then there's the walking. To buy groceries or get to the subway, the bus, the pharmacy, or the movie theater, you'd have to walk up a steep hill to Broadway. West 72nd Street, a main shopping area, was at least a mile away. It was probably a mile walk to meet my best friend Trudy Smoke on 88th and West End Avenue. When I taught at the Calhoun School on 74th Street or at the Heschel School on 89th Street or visited my grandmother or my mother on 73rd Street, I walked. We all walked, miles every day.

Fires, floods, sinkings, and growing old never stopped our tough little group of liveaboards. In the end, it was failing infrastructure that brought on the community's demise. In the spring of 2021, the New York City Parks Department announced it was closing the Boat Basin. The marina had been deemed unsafe, and all of the boats had to leave by the first of November.[1]

It was true the marina was worn out, following decades of neglect. It had not been dredged in over sixty years. At low tide, all of the boats sat in muck, and the window to take a boat out or bring one in had shrunk to just a few hours a day. The wooden docks and pilings had fallen victim to devastating nor'easters, Hurricanes Irene and Sandy, wood-eating shipworms, and tiny crustaceans called "gribbles." If only the parks department had handled the situation differently by adding more docks for recreational boaters and taking better care of the marina itself. But plans to increase docks for recreational boats had never come to fruition. Every boating season, fewer and fewer slips were occupied, even though there were many hundreds of people on the waiting list. In fact, before the marina closed, there were almost one thousand names on a fourteen-year-long waiting list to get a slip.

This all speaks to such poor management and no vision of what a floating community could be. Cities around the world and here in the United States—Seattle, Washington, Sausalito, California, and Washington, D.C.—allow people who love the water to live on boats. The city's planned renovation following the eviction of the Boat Basin residents promised a fully dredged marina and concrete docks—nine of them, instead of the original five. I found myself wondering if the parks department would allow year-round residents, but given the history of vilification, it seemed unlikely. Will the Boat Basin ever again be a vibrant community filled with people from different continents, socioeconomic strata, professions, and ages?

When Henry Stern was parks commissioner, he called us squatters. Yet, it was our community that kept the marina open in the winter for decades and made it a thriving and popular site along the river. In a *Gothamist* interview in January 2022, Gale Brewer, a longtime ally of the Boat Basin liveaboards, a former Manhattan borough president, and an Upper West Side city council member for many years, said, "What makes it special is the liveaboards. You can have a marina and that's nice, there are marinas all around the city. But the fact that it is a home for people . . . that's why it's unique. It's all about the liveaboards."[2]

Many times since 2021, I have ridden in a cab past the old Boat Basin. No one and nothing is there except for the docks, the gulls, some mallard ducks, and pigeons. A ghost town.

The fate and future of the marina as a community might be in the hands of the local community board: Manhattan Community Board 7—a powerful city advisory board made up of community members that represent the Upper West Side from Columbus Circle to West 110th Street, Central Park to the Hudson River. At the Community Board 7 meeting held on June 17, 2024, the architects of the marina presented their updated plans. The meeting ended with a resolution regarding the future of the marina:

Re: West 79th Street Marina and Dock house, on the proposed design.

The following facts and concerns were considered in arriving at our conclusion:

On June 17, 2024, the NYC Department of Parks and Recreation and the NYC Economic Development Corporation, along with their design and engineering partners (collectively, the "Agencies") presented a comprehensive plan (the "Plan") for the reconstruction of the West 79th Street Dockhouse (the "Dockhouse") and Marina.

In 2019, the Agencies announced a comprehensive expansion and redesign of the Dockhouse and Marina. The goals of the Plan included: (1) climate-resilient design; (2) upgrade to modern codes and design; (3) ADA-accessibility; (4) accommodating the 1000+ waitlist of boaters awaiting slips at the Marina; (5) full utilities connectivity to City infrastructure; and (6) enhanced programming for users, like children. Subsequently, the Agencies presented three evolving design schematics to Community Board 7 ("CB7") before their latest presentation.

The response to these three prior designs was largely negative. The objections included: (1) The aesthetic "look and feel" of the Dockhouse, including the increased size and height of the structure and a modern style that seemed, to many, alien to the historic nature of the Riverside Park setting; (2) The expansion of the Marina; and (3) The potentially obstructed visibility of the Hudson River and landmarks like the George Washington Bridge from Riverside Park.

On June 17, 2024, the Agencies returned to our committee with a design that is the most evolved so far, though not final. It is comprised of:

- A 3,800 sqft Dockhouse that is on the Hudson River/77th street.
- An enlarged marina by the Dockhouse that will be able to accommodate 193 vessels.
- Dredging for navigable depths and future expansion of two potential docks.
- Full connectivity of all utilities to the City's infrastructure—water, electric and sewage—for the first time in the Dockhouse and Marina's history.
- Installation of a wave screen outside new Marine structures.

While not perfect, CB7 believes that the revised design represents a fair compromise. The Dockhouse is still considered overly large by some, but it is certainly smaller than the 6,175 sq ft structure that was proposed originally. The height may still be imposing, but the Dockhouse will have a green roof and will be located two blocks south of 79th street, thereby not spoiling the views from the Rotunda. The size of the marina is being expanded significantly, but this will allow the City to address the 1000+ waitlist for slips.

Further, CB7 believes that benefits to the community from the execution of the Plan include full ADA-accessibility of the Marina Project, a LEED-standard Dockhouse, expanded programming for children of all ages and abilities, dockmasters, etc, full connectivity to the City infrastructure for the first time in the Marina's history, and of course, climate and flood resilience for decades to come.

Despite this, CB7 acknowledges that many community members remain dissatisfied with the Plan, for various reasons. **THEREFORE, BE IT RESOLVED** that Community Board 7 / Manhattan **SUPPORTS** the Plan as presented, with the following recommendations:

- The built-up area of the Dockhouse may not be increased.
- Elements of nature should guide any design changes.
- Recreational vessels or cruises that contribute to excessive noise and pollution should not be allowed.
- Marine education programming should be expanded for all ages and abilities.
- **Any members of the live-aboard community that existed at the Marina prior to 2021, who want to return once the Marina is renovated, must receive priority in relocation back at the Marina.**[3]

This resolution gives me great hope. Whether my former neighbors are allowed to return to the Boat Basin remains to be seen, but just hearing that last bullet point read at the meeting was a tremendous show of support from the men and women of the Community Board of the Upper West Side.

Before I was ready to leave the marina, just the thought of moving away filled me with unutterable sadness and dread. The experience of being surrounded by the natural world, with views of our sparkling city, is one that will never leave me. The friendships, connections, and bonds that I have with the Boat Basin community are precious. Thinking of some of my longtime neighbors, many of them in their eighties, being forced to leave the marina that had been their home for more than fifty years—it must have been unbearable.

To have been able to live most of my own adult life on the water was a dream come true. The river was where I found my soulmate, where we raised our child, and where I discovered my calling in life. It was where I was meant to be, and I am forever grateful for having that opportunity. Because of those many golden years, and because of the people and animals and plants of and along the river, I am all the richer. I share this wealth through my books, my talks, and my classes.

I am not a religious woman, not in an organized way, but I am deeply spiritual when it comes to nature, the source of all love and life. Living on a boat, attuned to flood and ebb tides, the phases of the moon, the calls of birds, sunrise and sunset, living with the power of wind and the sound of rain, surrounded by people who cared about each other—all of it, all of it touched me to my soul and forever changed me.

Living on a boat is not for everyone, but it is for those of us who love the water. I love looking at it, swimming in it, watching sunsets reflected in its glassy surface, feeling my home bob gently in a summer breeze, or rocking violently during a blizzard. Living on a boat made us feel connected to the power of nature.

Our little summer house in the Catskills is near the Schoharie, a mountain river that empties into the Hudson. For many seasons, I swam in that beautiful river, but when we'd come home on Sunday afternoons and cross the George Washington Bridge, I'd look down on the mighty Hudson and say to my family, "Now *that's* a river."

Perhaps someday the 79th Street Boat Basin will once again be a floating community and, in the words of my former neighbor, Simone Di Bagno, one of the few magical villages of the world.

Figure 46. Leslie's first swim in the Hudson, 1998.

Returning

In 2019, I joined a pool in a building in Riverdale, where I stopped to swim each morning on my way home from driving my granddaughter to the Hudson Lab School in Hastings-On-Hudson. For two years I had been looking at apartments in that beautiful building and imagining what my dream apartment would have—a terrace on a high floor with a view of the river and the Palisades.

On a Saturday morning in early September 2021, my dream apartment materialized. Two months later, we moved in. If I look southwest to the Palisades in Englewood Cliffs, I can see the area where I lived as a child. While memories of some things are fading, I still clearly remember the colors of the eastern sky at dawn and the sun-dappled water. Once again, I wake up to the Hudson. From my twenty-third-floor window, I can see from the George Washington Bridge to the Tappan Zee Bridge. Below me is Seton Park, Raoul Wallenberg Forest, Riverdale Park, the Palisades, and the great river flowing by it all.

Figure 47. View from Leslie's apartment window in Riverdale: the river, the *Clearwater*, and the Palisades, October 10, 2024.

EPILOGUE

River Resources

The following list—by no means exhaustive—highlights some of the Hudson River education and outreach programs that have been developed over the years. I am grateful to know that their work will help ensure good stewardship of my beloved river in the years to come.

CURB: Center for the Urban River at Beczak

In September 2019, Jonah and I were invited to the Hudson Lab School, where my granddaughter Aya attended kindergarten. The school sits on twenty-five acres above the Hudson in the historic town of Hastings-on-Hudson. It is located on the lower level of a nursing home called Andrus on Hudson. This proximity allows for both intergenerational learning with the "grands," the residents of Andrus, and the study of the natural world, including the river below.

Figure 48. Leslie's granddaughter, Aya (*second from right*), seining with her kindergarten class, helped by college students at CURB, the Sarah Lawrence College Center for the Urban River at Beczak, Yonkers, New York, 2019.

That year, the school had only been established for three years, the entire school—twenty-seven children, grades kindergarten through sixth grade—was studying the Hudson. The teachers thought it would be interesting for their students to learn about what it was like to live on the river, hence the invitation to me and my son. During our visit, we were interviewed by a number of children, and we also joined them for some of their learning activities.

As part of the latter, my granddaughter and her classmates went seining in the river with student interns from Sarah Lawrence College at the Center for the Urban River at Beczak (CURB). That day, the sky and the river were a deep blue. There were no waves and no whitecaps. The water was warm, the summer's heat still trapped within. One by one, the kids stepped into child-size hip waders and held the pole of one side of the seine net, assisted by a Sarah Lawrence student. I longed to walk into the river with the children. Watching them, I could again feel the river's pressure against my hip waders, the sensation of sinking into the river bottom. I recalled the joyful anticipation of discovering what animals we'd find in the net, getting to look closely at each one, and learning something about them.

With the help of the net and the college students, the children herded fish, crabs, and shrimp onto the little beach. Their catch that morning included silversides, small fish with shiny silver stripes; a goby, a small bottom-feeder; a young striped bass; shore shrimp; and young blue crabs. The silversides, goby, blue crabs, and shrimp were carried back to the Hudson Lab School's classrooms where tanks and food (frozen blood worms) awaited them. The rest were measured and returned to the river.

CURB is an environmental center that sits on the shores of the Hudson in Yonkers. The center has direct access to a tidal marsh, a beach used for seining, and a fully outfitted field station laboratory. There, the Sarah Lawrence students record river data daily: air and water temperature, weather conditions, bacteria levels, and the number of caught fish and aquatic invertebrates and their measurements. They share this data with the New York State Department of Environmental Conservation and other regional partners.[1] In addition, CURB has installed a Hudson River Environmental Conditions Observing System (HRECOS) at the nearby Science Barge.[2] It is one of a network of dozens of stations stretching from New York City to Albany. The system records and monitors river data such as temperature, pH, salinity, dissolved oxygen, chlorophyll, and turbidity.

The Science Barge

I first saw the Science Barge when it was docked near the 79th Street Boat Basin off Riverside Park South at Pier I in 2007. Powered by wind turbines and solar panels, the Science Barge is a floating urban farm that utilizes hydroponics to grow vegetables with collected rainwater and desalinated Hudson River water. It was designed by Ted Caplow, a pioneer in urban agriculture, who also founded NY Sun Works, a not-for-profit that builds hydroponic classrooms. As of 2024, they have designed and built three

Figure 49. The Science Barge on the Hudson River moored off
Riverside Park South, 2007.

hundred hydroponic classrooms in all five boroughs of New York City.[3]
The summer the barge was near the Boat Basin, I toured it many times.
I thought this floating urban farm was a marvel. The healthy plants were
producing tons of little tomatoes, green peppers, and lettuce. It was beautiful inside the floating greenhouse. In 2008, the Science Barge was sold
to Groundwork Hudson Valley in the City of Yonkers for $2.00, and it
remains open to school visits during the week and to the public on the
weekends.

Groundwork Hudson Valley was created to bring environmental justice to poor communities in the lower Hudson Valley. The barge works
with the Get Fresh Yonkers Farm Co-Op, the Yonkers Farmers' Market,
and community-supported agriculture. On the barge, food is grown with
no agricultural waste, no carbon emissions, and no pesticides. The Science
Barge works with educators in order "to empower the next generation of
environmental leaders." It has virtual classes for teachers and children and
in-person tours and classes.[4]

The Clearwater's Sailing Classroom

Once A Day in the Life of the Hudson started taking place, my school booked trips on the *Clearwater* to coincide with that event. It was always an awesome experience for children and teachers alike to be part of the crew of this magnificent sloop, with the wind at our backs and the huge sails fully open. The experience of being out on the water with the Palisades to the west was exhilarating.

Once on board, the children would learn about the history of the ship and the history of the river. They would get to steer the sloop and raise and lower the sails. Scientists and environmental educators on board would help the children lower nets to collect animals, bring the nets up, and put the animals in small tanks. Then they would use a dichotomous key created by the Clearwater to identify the common Hudson River fish and learn about their lives.[5] The children would get to do water quality tests and record the data.[6]

Figure 50. The Elisabeth Morrow School's fifth grade students collecting data on board the *Clearwater* during its A Day in the Life of the Hudson event, October 2011.

Columbia University's Lamont-Doherty Earth Observatory

Columbia University's Lamont-Doherty Earth Observatory (LDEO) in Palisades, New York, has a Hudson River program created by Margie Turrin and run by Margie and her colleague Marisa Annunziato, with programs attracting communities, teachers, adults, and children from the surrounding areas of Rockland, Bergen, Westchester, Bronx, and New York counties. Their free Science Saturday program, held from July through September, takes participants of all ages seining and teaches them how to identify the fish they catch and how to test the water quality of the river. Using microscopes, participants learn how to identify the smaller life forms of the river's zooplankton and phytoplankton. Seeing these tiny creatures living on the algae was always an unforgettable experience for me and my students. Seining and using a microscope are the best ways to see who lives beneath the surface of the river without harming those enchanting creatures.

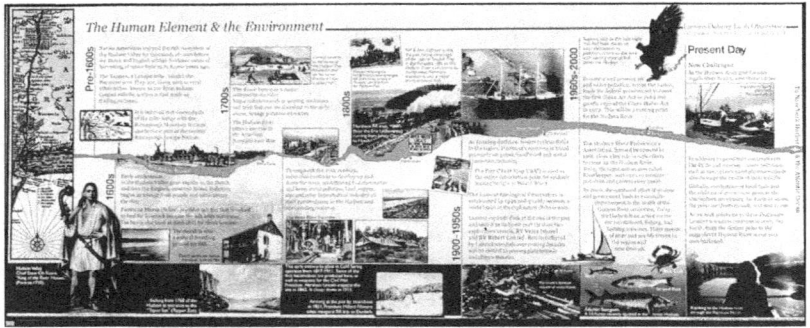

Figure 51. Mural depicting the history of the river at the Lamont-Doherty Earth Observatory's Hudson River Field Station, Piermont, New York.

The LDEO also has a fully equipped indoor lab in their Hudson River Field Station in Piermont, New York, at the river's edge, where kindergarten through twelfth grade students, teachers, student teachers, and graduate students learn that the river is not "dirty" but that its color is the product of a richness of microscopic life and their food source.[7] Margie explained this so beautifully:

If you think about it this way: in animals, respiration is the process in the body by which the organic nutrients are oxidized or broken down to release energy. In the Hudson it is the breaking down of detritus that provides the energy into the system. This is what makes it so important for newly spawned and young of year fish. There is some plant and algal life photo-synthesizing, but it is far outweighed by the detritus, nutrients and miner-als from the tributaries. There are many causes of the murky coloration, all part of its richness as an estuary is the mix of the fine bottom sediments and the suspended materials—for example, the sediments and detritus washing in from the surrounding watershed, phytoplankton and zooplankton are in the top one-third or so, and even salt in the lower section of the estuary cre-ates a tension as it moves in and out of solution.[8]

Students spending time at the field station learn observation skills as they notice the currents and tides and identify the animals they catch in the seine net. They learn how to test the chemistry of the river and how to share data with scientists who are studying the Hudson at the New York Department of Conservation and at Cornell University.

In a handout for high school students on the LDEO's website, you'll find this poetry:

Each of us has a *water address*. No matter where you reside on land, you are a part of a watershed. A *watershed* is a geographic area whose rain-fall, snowmelt, streams, and rivers all flow or drain into a common body of water, such as an ocean, lake, river, stream, estuary, or reservoir. Ultimately, most watersheds eventually drain into the ocean. At Lamont-Doherty Earth Observatory's Field Station, we are a part of the Hudson River watershed, one of particular importance as it expands across approximately a third of New York State and even into New Jersey, Vermont, Massachusetts and Connecticut! The freshwater input of the Hudson River starts at any loca-tion within the watershed. One drop of rainwater in the watershed could contribute towards the freshwater of the Hudson River, eventually draining into the Atlantic Ocean.[9]

A Day in the Life of the Hudson

Margie Turrin of LDEO and Chris Bowser of the New York Department of Environmental Conservation's Hudson River Estuary Program run the successful program A Day in the Life of the Hudson each October, where more than five thousand students travel to 105 locations on the river, stretching from Staten Island to Troy, 153 miles north of the harbor at the upper end of the Hudson River estuary.[10] The children and their teachers become scientists that day, conducting labs in the field. They learn how to use a hydrometer to measure the amount of salt in the water and the Beaufort Wind Scale chart for measuring the effects of wind speed on the river. They learn how to use chemical test kits and digital probes to measure dissolved oxygen in the water, an important determinant for animal life in the river. Fish, crabs, and all the animals of the river need oxygen, just like we do. The amount of dissolved oxygen in the water indicates the health of the river and its animals. The river receives oxygen through diffusion from the air and through turbulence caused by wind against the river's surface. Students take the temperature of the air and water and learn how to use a Secchi disk to measure turbidity, which is caused by sediment—the sand, silt, and mud carried in by the ocean, streams, and tributaries that are part of the Hudson River watershed. Turbidity is also due to the presence of phytoplankton, zooplankton, and detritus—the dead plant and animal material that is food for zooplankton and animals like the oyster, who filter the river water.[11]

Hudson River Estuary Program

Scientists and educators at the LDEO also work closely with the Hudson River Estuary Program (HREP) of the New York Department of Environmental Conservation, the accomplished state entity, whose goal is to protect the river and its wildlife.

In an action agenda found on the New York State Department of Environmental Conservation's website, you'll read that their goal for 2025 and beyond is to "conserve, protect, and enhance river and shoreline habitats to assure that life cycles of key species are supported to sustain a healthy ecosystem." This includes rebuilding and protecting oyster beds and removing dams and barriers that stop migratory fish, such as herring and eels, from reaching their spawning grounds.[12]

The HREP has a website that lists Hudson River lesson plans and professional development workshops for teachers, free field education programs for middle school, high school, and college students, and citizen science projects for up and down the river. Tom Lake's *Hudson River Almanac* is also part of this important program.[13]

Billion Oyster Project

The Billion Oyster Project has heavily invested in training teachers in person and online.[14] They have a rich collection of online curricula and teaching aids like their beautiful *Species Identification Guide* with gorgeous watercolor paintings of fish and aquatic invertebrates: oysters, crabs, clams, shrimp, and snails. They sponsor over fifty oyster research field stations throughout the five boroughs where volunteers can monitor oysters, count and measure them, and relay the data. The Billion Oyster Project encourages people with access to New York City's waters to create their own research station.[15]

It is up to you, dear reader, to keep learning about our natural world. I promise you, your life will be all the richer for it.

Figure 52. Oyster larvae attach themselves to any hard surface, including clamshells, and continue to grow into small oysters, called spat.

ACKNOWLEDGMENTS

To my former neighbors, the 79th Street Boat Basin diaspora—my love goes out to you wherever you are, especially to Ed Bacon who held our fragile community together for so many decades. This book is dedicated to all of you.

As a teacher of the river, I have had the opportunity to meet and work with brilliant people who are knowledgeable about the Hudson. They include Margie Turrin of Columbia University's Lamont-Doherty Earth Observatory, who helped immeasurably with this book by reading different versions and setting me straight when I had erred. Tom Lake, who reviewed this book for accuracy, is the author of the *Hudson River Almanac* and a teacher of the river who would show up in my classroom and on the beach below the Palisades once each year to work with my students identifying the fish and aquatic invertebrates, tides, and currents of the river. Christopher Letts was also there on these visits and would don hip waders with me so we could seine the river. Oh, it was a scary but wonderful experience each and every time to sink into that "black mayonnaise" riverbed and then herd the animals in the net back to the beach, never knowing what living treasures we would find. Peter Malinowsky, cofounder and director of the Billion Oyster Project, reviewed the chapters on oysters and the work of his organization. I am a huge fan of his dedication to protecting the river.

My seventeen years as a science teacher at The Elisabeth Morrow School in Englewood, New Jersey, were the greatest of my professional career. The head of our school, David Lowry, and the principal, Germaine DiPaolo, let me soar as a teacher. They supported my having animals in the classroom—over seventy—including fish, amphibians, reptiles, birds, mammals, and all kinds of invertebrates. We had a greenhouse and a koi pond, and outside was a garden. They even let me bring my dog, Sadie, to school. The wonderful teachers and staff I worked with became my dear friends: Sanda Cohen, Nancy Dorrien, Gil Marino, Carolyn Milne, Lisa Nicolau, Eleanor Schuster, Gail Weeks, and Gail Winter, just to name a few.

Thank you to the talented photographers and artists who let me use their beautiful photos and drawings: Beth Bergman, Cindy Kane, Jessica Maffia, Eric Nelsen and the Palisades Interstate Park Commission, Gloria Nelson, Jonah Nishiura, Trudy Smoke, and Rolando Yera. And with the help of P. J. Sieswerda and Catherine McClave of Gotham Whale, I discovered Artie Raslich's powerful whale photos.

In 2019, I reached out to Kitty Liu, editor at Cornell University Press, with my idea to write a book about the Hudson: part memoir, part human and natural history of the river that runs through my life. I am eternally grateful for her patience and guidance. This book never would have been written without her support. Thank you to Kitty's capable assistant, India Miraglia, for her help. A huge thank you to Mary Kate Murphy, my immensely talented copyeditor at Cornell. She is a marvel.

To my brilliant friend of more than sixty years and the illustrator of several of my books, including *River*, Trudy Smoke, thank you, thank you for your love and support. How I've loved working on these projects with you. And thanks to Trudy's husband and my friend, Alan Robbins, who has helped design so many of these projects.

My dear neighbors and friends in the Whitehall Building's green spaces committee, writers circle, book club, artists group, and intergenerational committee, who have welcomed me into a creative, loving community in Riverdale deserve recognition: John Andreotti, Shirley Bender, Jackie

Biaggi, Gerald Brody, Anna Cantor, Myrna Cruz, Len and Emily Daykin, Aliza Erber, John Finch, Danny Fitzgibbon, Julie Gaynor, Chana Gutreiman, Joan Hollander, Marilyn Howard, Jeffrey Klapper, Lisa Marum, Iris Phillips, Laura Pucher, Celeste Ramirez, Penny and Sidney Rosenblatt, Sabina and Alex Rosenblum, Lenny Silverberg, Sarah Steinhardt, Dave Turkheimer, and Laura Wolner.

To my family: thank you to my dear husband of now forty-eight years, Jim, who helped me find my true path, helped our community survive when the city tried to destroy it, and helped create a magical lifestyle living on boats. Thank you to our dear son, Jonah, who continues to bring such happiness into our lives and who is always there for us as we navigate old age, and to the magnificent human that is his wife, Gina Auletta, my North Star. And of course, thank you to the joy of our lives, our granddaughter, Aya Moon Nishiura. I love you all.

NOTES

1. What the Water Holds

1. Robert A. M. Stern, Gregory Gilmartin, and Thomas Mellins, *New York 1930: Architecture and Urbanism Between the Two World Wars* (New York: Rizzoli, 1987), 677–79.

2. Robert H. Boyle, *The Hudson River: A Natural and Unnatural History* (New York: W. W. Norton, 1979), 26–28.

3. E. Emory Davis and Eric Nelsen, *New Jersey's Palisades Interstate Park* (Charleston, SC: Arcadia Library Editions, 2007), 43–48.

4. Jeanne Haffner, "The Palisades in Peril: Meet the Forgotten Women Who Fought to Save the Great Cliffs of the Hudson River," The New-York Historical, April 30, 2019, https://www.nyhistory.org/blogs/palisades-peril-forgotten-women-saved.

5. "19th Century and the Perkins Legacy," Wave Hill, accessed July 18, 2024, https://www.wavehill.org/discover/our-mission-history/19th-century-and-the-perkins-legacy.

6. "19th Century and the Perkins Legacy."

7. Robert O. Binnewies, *Palisades: The People's Park*, 2nd ed. (New York: Fordham University Press, 2021), 19–21.

8. "The Palisades," Fort Tryon Park Trust, accessed July 17, 2024, https://www.forttryonparktrust.org/the-palisades/.

9. "A History of Film in Fort Lee, NJ," Barrymore Film Center, accessed July 17, 2024, www.barrymorefilmcenter.com/history.

10. Davis and Nelsen, *New Jersey's Palisades Interstate Park*, 26.

11. Ann Lund, "Undercliff Cemetery/Whack Me Jug Grave, Englewood Cliffs NY," *FreeHiddenWorld (Exploring Local NY/NJ History)*, June 28, 2020, freehiddenworld.word press.com/2020/06/28/undercliff-cemetery-whack-me-jug-grave.

12. Davis and Nelsen, *New Jersey's Palisades Interstate Park*, 60.

13. "Yonkers, New York," National Park Service, accessed July 17, 2024, https://www. nps.gov/articles/000/yonkers-new-york.htm.

14. Bill A3183, Assembly No. 3183, State of New Jersey, 216th Legislature (2014), https://www.njleg.state.nj.us/bill-search/2014/A3183/bill-text?f=A3500&n=3183_I1.

15. "Exploring Nature at the Palisades Interstate Park in New Jersey," Palisades Interstate Park Commission, accessed July 17, 2024, www.njpalisades.org/nature.html.

16. Jim Dwyer, "LG to Reduce Height of Headquarters, Preserving Palisades Horizon," *New York Times*, June 23, 2015, www.nytimes.com/2015/06/24/nyregion/lg-to-reduce-height-of-headquarters-preserving-palisades-horizon.html.

2. Homecoming

1. Elizabeth Knowles, ed., *The Oxford Dictionary of Phrase and Fable*, 2nd ed. (Oxford: Oxford University Press, 2005), under "mandala."

2. Stephen P. Stanne, Roger G. Panetta, and Brian E. Forist, *The Hudson: An Illustrated Guide to the Living River* (New Brunswick, NJ: Rutgers University Press, 1996), 6.

3. Eric W. Sanderson and Markley Boyer, *Mannahatta: A Natural History of New York City* (New York: Abrams, 2009), 143.

4. "Andrew Haswell Green," The New York Preservation Archive Project, accessed July 23, 2024, www.nypap.org/preservation-history/andrew-haswell-green/.

5. Robert A. Caro, *The Power Broker: Robert Moses and the Fall of New York* (New York: Alfred A. Knopf, 1974), 65.

6. Peggy Gavan, "1933: Herbert Hoover and Andy Mellon, the Pet Pigs of Camp Thomas Paine," *The Hatching Cat of Gotham: True and Unusual Animal Tales of Old New York*, January 4, 2021, https://hatchingcatnyc.com/2021/01/04/pet-pigs-camp-thomas-paine/.

7. Gavan, "1933: Herbert Hoover and Andy Mellon."

8. E. L. Danvers, "A Shanty Town Along the Hudson River," *I Love the Upper West Side*, last modified April 4, 2023, ilovetheupperwestside.com/a-shanty-town-along-the-hudson-river/#google_vignette.

9. Lucie Levine, "Looking Back at the Depression-Era Shanty Towns in New York City Parks," 6sqft, February 26, 2020, https://www.6sqft.com/looking-back-at-the-depression-era-shanty-towns-in-new-york-city-parks/.

10. "Squatters Must Leave. Moses Orders Camp Thomas Paine on Hudson Vacated by May 1," *New York Times*, April 18, 1934, timesmachine.nytimes.com/times machine/1934/04/18/97142604.html?pageNumber=7.

11. Ed Bacon, *Boat Basin BULLetin*, no. 7 (December 2008), http://all-nyc-yachts.com/BOAT%20BASIN%20BULLetin%20-%20Issue%207.pdf.

3. Student, Teacher

1. Angèle Sancho Passe, *Is Everybody Ready for Kindergarten?: A Toolkit for Preparing Children and Families* (St. Paul, MN: Redleaf Press, 2010), 42.

2. "Where We Started," The Elisabeth Morrow School, accessed July 17, 2024, https://elisabethmorrow.org/block-slider/the-history-of-ems/.

3. Stephen P. Stanne, Roger G. Panetta, and Brian E. Forist, *The Hudson: An Illustrated Guide to the Living River* (New Brunswick, NJ: Rutgers University Press, 1996), 6–9.

4. Bob Berman, "What Are Spring Tides & Neap Tides?" *Almanac*, November 30, 2023, https://www.almanac.com/what-are-spring-tides-neap-tides.

5. Christopher J. Schuberth, *The Geology of New York City and Environs* (Garden City, NY: The Natural History Press, 1968), 180.

6. Betsy McCully, "Ice Age History: How Glaciers Shaped New York," New York Nature, updated August 25, 2023, https://www.newyorknature.us/ice-age-new-york/; William J. Broad, "How the Ice Age Shaped New York," *New York Times*, June 5, 2018, https://www.nytimes.com/2018/06/05/science/how-the-ice-age-shaped-new-york.html.

7. David Levine, "The Flood That Created the Hudson Valley," *Times Union*, July 16, 2023, https://www.timesunion.com/hudsonvalley/article/flood-ice-age-glacial-lake-iroquois-18199700.php.

8. Robert J. Dineen and William B. Rogers, "Sedimentary Environments in Glacial Lake Albany in the Albany Section of the Hudson-Champlain Lowlands," paper in the guidebook for the Joint Annual Meeting of the New York State Geological Association 51st Annual Meeting and the New England Intercollegiate Geological Conference 71st Meeting, Troy, NY, October 5–7, 1979: 87–199, https://www.nysga-online.org/wp-content/uploads/2019/06/NYSGA-1979-A3-Sedimentary-Environments-In-Glacial-Lake-Albany-In-The-Albany-Section-Of-The-Hudson-Champlain-Lowlands.pdf.

9. Schuberth, *The Geology of New York City and Environs,* 176–77.

10. "Our Tribal History . . . ," The Nanticoke Lenni-Lenape: An American Indian Tribe, accessed July 17, 2024, https://nanticoke-lenape.info/history.htm#:~:text=We%20called%20ourselves%20%22Lenni%2DLenape.

11. Eric W. Sanderson and Markley Boyer, *Mannahatta: A Natural History of New York City* (New York: Abrams, 2009), 153.

12. Samuel Eliot Morison, "The Sea in Literature," *The Atlantic*, September 1, 1955, https://www.theatlantic.com/magazine/archive/1955/09/the-sea-in-literature/641300/#.

13. Arthur James Weise, *The Discoveries of America to the Year 1525* (New York: G. P. Putnam's Sons, 1884), 308, https://www.gutenberg.org/cache/epub/67766/pg67766-images.html#CHAPTER_IX.

14. John Thorne, "Henry Hudson and the Half Moon, 1609," Gotham History, May 12, 2015, https://gothamhistory.com/2015/05/12/henry-hudson-and-the-half-moon-1609/; "Early Descriptions of New Netherland," New Netherland Institute, accessed February 2, 2025, https://www.newnetherlandinstitute.org/history-and-heritage/additional-resources/dutch-treats/early-impressions-of-new-netherland.

15. Adriaen van der Donck, *A Description of New Netherland,* ed. Charles T. Gehring and William A. Starna, trans. Diederik W. Goedhuys (Lincoln: University of Nebraska Press, 2010), Kindle location 253.

16. "Minetta Green," New York City Department of Parks and Recreation, accessed July 12, 2024, https://www.nycgovparks.org/parks/minetta-green/history.

17. Sanderson and Boyer, *Mannahatta,* 153.

18. Tricia Kang, "What Lies Beneath: A History of Collect Pond," Tenement Museum, accessed July 12, 2024, https://www.tenement.org/blog/what-lies-beneath-a-history-of-collect-pond/.

19. Eric Sanderson, "Recreating Mannahatta," The Welikia Project, accessed July 29, 2024, https://welikia.org/science/recreating-mannahatta/.

20. Robert H. Boyle, *The Hudson River: A Natural and Unnatural History* (New York: W. W. Norton, 1979), 15–16.

21. Boyle, *The Hudson River*, 102.

22. "Hudson River Fish Advisory Outreach Project," New York State Department of Health, accessed July 29, 2024, https://www.health.ny.gov/environmental/outdoors/fish/hudson_river/advisory_outreach_project/.

23. Linda Greenhouse, "Pollution Accusations Against G.M. Dismay North Tarrytown," *New York Times*, January 12, 1971, https://www.nytimes.com/1971/01/12/archives/pollution-accusations-against-gm-dismay-north-tarrytown.html.

24. "The Sloop," Hudson River Sloop Clearwater, accessed July 29, 2024, https://www.clearwater.org/the-sloop/.

25. Richard J. Langlois, "The Hudson River Sloop Clearwater: Sailing to Save the River," Hudson River Valley Institute, accessed February 2, 2025, https://www.hudsonrivervalley.org/sloop-clearwater#:~:text=Many%20of%20Clearwater's%20passengers%20are,sloop!"%20said%20Captain%20Flynn.

26. "History of the Clean Water Act," United States Environmental Protection Agency, last updated June 12, 2024, https://www.epa.gov/laws-regulations/history-clean-water-act.

27. Edward Hudson, "City's Largest Sewage Plant Is Going upon the Hudson," *New York Times*, September 2, 1972, https://timesmachine.nytimes.com/timesmachine/1972/09/02/81957590.pdf?pdf_redirect=true&ip=0.

28. "New York City's Wastewater Treatment System," New York City Department of Environmental Protection, accessed July 29, 2024, https://semspub.epa.gov/work/02/206372.pdf.

4. River Life

1. Hilary Hutcheson, "Managing Menhaden: The Most Important Fish in the Sea," *Fly Fisherman*, May 25, 2021, https://www.flyfisherman.com/editorial/menhaden-most-important-fish-in-sea/392897; Karl Vilacoba, "Ocean Story #8: In Gotham City, a Dark Sight Rises," Mid-Atlantic Ocean Data Portal, accessed July 17, 2024, https://portal.midatlantic ocean.org/ocean-stories/gotham-whale-new-york-humpbacks/.

2. Stephen P. Stanne, Roger G. Panetta, and Brian E. Forist, *The Hudson: An Illustrated Guide to the Living River* (New Brunswick, NJ: Rutgers University Press, 1996), 60.

3. "Fishing Gear: Purse Seines," NOAA (National Oceanic and Atmospheric Administration) Fisheries, accessed July 29, 2024, https://www.fisheries.noaa.gov/national/bycatch/fishing-gear-purse-seines.

4. Tom Schlichter, "Governor Cuomo Signs Bill to Protect Menhaden," *Outdoor Tom*, April 18, 2019, http://outdoortom.com/2019/04/5488/.

5. "The Return of the Most Important Fish in the Sea," The Nature Conservancy, February 12, 2020, https://www.nature.org/en-us/about-us/where-we-work/united-states/new-york/stories-in-new-york/menhaden-whales-return-new-york/.

6. Oliver Milman, "'They Are Amazed': New York City Sees Extraordinary Leap in Whale Sightings," *The Guardian*, June 3, 2019, https://www.theguardian.com/us-news/2019/jun/03/new-york-city-whale-sightings-increase.

7. J. L. Ripley, "Differential Parental Nutrient Allocation in Two Congeneric Pipefish Species (Syngnathidae: *Syngnathus* Spp.)," *Journal of Experimental Biology* 209, no. 6 (March 15, 2006): 1112–21, https://doi.org/10.1242/jeb.02119.

8. Carl Zimmer, "How Flounder Wound Up with an Epic Side-Eye," *New York Times*, June 21, 2024, https://www.nytimes.com/2024/06/21/science/flounder-flatfish-evolution.html.

9. Ruth Heller, *A Sea Within a Sea: Secrets of the Sargasso* (New York: Grosset & Dunlap, 2000), 26–27; "What is the Sargasso Sea?," National Ocean Service, accessed July 29, 2024, https://oceanservice.noaa.gov/facts/sargassosea.html.

10. "American Eel," US Fish and Wildlife Service, accessed July 29, 2024, https://www.fws.gov/species/american-eel-anguilla-rostrata; Stanne, Panetta, and Forist, *The Hudson*, 69.

11. Danielle Olson, "The Origin of Eels," Smithsonian Ocean, December 2022, https://ocean.si.edu/ocean-life/fish/origin-eels.

12. Jamie Baldwin and Sönke Johnsen, "The Importance of Color in Mate Choice of the Blue Crab *Callinectes sapidus*," *Journal of Experimental Biology* 212, no. 22 (November 2009): 3762–68.

13. William W. Warner, *Beautiful Swimmers* (New York: Little, Brown, 1994), 90–119; "Hudson River Animal of the Month: Blue Crab," Center for the Urban River at Beczak, accessed July 29, 2024, https://www.centerfortheurbanriver.org/news-events/news/bluecrab-facts.html; Virginia Institute of Marine Science, "Swimming Blue Crab," May 10, 2017, YouTube, 36 sec., https://youtu.be/tzjKduvXz5Y?feature=shared.

14. Stanne, Panetta, and Forist, *The Hudson*, 59–60; Robert H. Boyle, *The Hudson River: A Natural and Unnatural History* (New York: W. W. Norton, 1979), 131–32; "Striped Bass," New York State Department of Environmental Conservation, accessed July 29, 2024, https://dec.ny.gov/nature/animals-fish-plants/hudson-delaware-marine-fisheries/striped-bass.

15. Dave Taft, "Striped Bass of the Hudson," *New York Times*, October 14, 2016, https://www.nytimes.com/2016/10/16/nyregion/striped-bass-of-the-hudson.html.

16. Hudson River Estuary Program, "Growing Up As a Striped Bass," New York State Department of Environmental Conservation, accessed July 29, 2024, https://extapps.dec.ny.gov/docs/remediation_hudson_pdf/hrlpk3sbass.pdf.

17. "Hudson Highlands: Part 1," New-York Historical Society, accessed July 29, 2024, https://hudsonrising.nyhistory.org/hudson-highlands-part-1/.

18. "Hudson Highlands: Part 1."

19. Reed Sparling, "The Shad Are Running—But for How Much Longer?," Scenic Hudson, accessed July 31, 2024, https://www.scenichudson.org/viewfinder/the-shad-are-running-but-for-how-much-longer/.

20. "Lenape Fishing," Official Web Site of the Delaware Tribe of Indians, June 27, 2013, https://delawaretribe.org/blog/2013/06/27/lenape-fishing/; John Conway, "Shad: The Founding Fish Returns," *New York Almanack*, May 13, 2014, https://www.newyorkalmanack.com/2014/05/shad-the-founding-fish-returns/; "The First People of the River," Riverkeeper, accessed July 29, 2024, https://www.riverkeeper.org/hudson-river/hudson-river-journey/the-first-people-of-the-river/.

21. Wes Eakin, Gregg Kenney, and ElizaBeth Streifeneder, "Recovery Plan for Hudson River American Shad," New York State Department of Environmental Conservation, Division of Marine Resources, March 2023, https://extapps.dec.ny.gov/docs/fish_marine_pdf/hudsonshadplan.pdf.

22. "Atlantic Sturgeon," NOAA Fisheries, accessed July 31, 2024, https://www.fisheries.noaa.gov/species/atlantic-sturgeon.

23. "Atlantic Sturgeon," New York State Department of Environmental Conservation, accessed July 31, 2024, https://dec.ny.gov/nature/animals-fish-plants/hudson-delaware-marine-fisheries/atlantic-sturgeon.

24. Stanne, Panetta, and Forist, *The Hudson*, 45.

25. Nate Schweber and Sharon Otterman, "A Painfully Early Arrival for a Summer Nuisance," *New York Times*, July 22, 2008, https://www.nytimes.com/2008/07/22/nyregion/22jellyfish.html.

26. "Lion's Mane Jellyfish," Oceana, accessed July 31, 2024, https://oceana.org/marine-life/lions-mane-jellyfish/.

27. John K. Terres, *The Audubon Society Encyclopedia of North American Birds* (Avenel, NJ: Wings Books, 1996), 106; Leslie Day, *Field Guide to the Natural World of New York City* (Baltimore: Johns Hopkins University Press, 2007), 168–69; Leslie Day, *Field Guide to the Neighborhood Birds of New York City* (Baltimore: Johns Hopkins University Press, 2015), 36–41.

28. Tod Winston, *New York City Audubon's Harbor Herons Project: 2021 Nesting Survey Report* (New York: New York City Audubon, 2021), https://www.hudsonriver.org/wp-content/uploads/2022/06/2021_HH_Interim_Survey_Report.pdf.

29. Leslie Day, *Field Guide to the Neighborhood Birds of New York City* (Baltimore: Johns Hopkins University Press, 2015), 19.

30. "History of the Christmas Bird Count," National Audubon Society, accessed July 18, 2024, https://www.audubon.org/community-science/christmas-bird-count/history-christmas-bird-count.

31. You can see this diorama here: American Museum of Natural History, "Birding at the Museum: Frank Chapman and the Dioramas," December 20, 2013, YouTube, 4 min., 9 sec., https://youtu.be/qb6j72hPC7E?feature=shared.

32. Terres, *Audubon Society Encyclopedia of North American Birds*, 272–73; Day, *Field Guide to the Natural World of New York City*, 198–99; Day, *Field Guide to the Neighborhood Birds of New York City*, 137, 140–43.

33. "Cadman Plaza Park," NYC Parks, accessed July 31, 2024, https://www.nycgov parks.org/parks/cadman-plaza-park-and-brooklyn-war-memorial/highlights/12535.

34. Rachel Carson, *Silent Spring*, 40th anniversary ed. (Boston: Houghton Mifflin, 2002).

35. John Kiernan, *Natural History of New York City* (New York: Houghton Mifflin, 1959), 243.

36. Terres, *Audubon Society Encyclopedia of North American Birds*, 477.

37. Terres, *Audubon Society Encyclopedia of North American Birds*, 644–46; Day, *Field Guide to the Natural World of New York City*, 196–97; Day, *Field Guide to the Neighborhood Birds of New York City*, 130–33.

38. Terres, *Audubon Society Encyclopedia of North American Birds*, 498; Day, *Field Guide to the Natural World of New York City*, 50, 85, 91, 110, 192–93; Day, *Field Guide to the Neighborhood Birds of New York City*, 89, 100–101.

39. Terres, *Audubon Society Encyclopedia of North American Birds*, 462; Day, *Field Guide to the Natural World of New York City*, 45; Day, *Field Guide to the Neighborhood Birds of New York City*, 74–77.

40. Terres, *Audubon Society Encyclopedia of North American Birds*, 462; Day, *Field Guide to the Natural World of New York City*, 45, 77; Day, *Field Guide to the Neighborhood Birds of New York City*, 78–81.

41. Terres, *Audubon Society Encyclopedia of North American Birds*, 460; Day, *Field Guide to the Natural World of New York City*, 45, 58; Day, *Field Guide to the Neighborhood Birds of New York City*, 73, 82–85.

42. Suzanne Charlé, "The Javits Center: Leading from the Rooftops," NYC Bird Alliance, accessed July 31, 2024, https://nycbirdalliance.org/blog/the-javits-center-leading-from-the-rooftops.

43. Judith Holzer et al., *Wickers Creek Archaeological Site: What You Should Know*, 2nd ed. (Dobbs Ferry, NY: The Friends of Wickers Creek Archaeological Site, 2005), http://75.103.101.60/documents/curriculum_speigelman_Friends_of_Wickers_Creek_Analysis.pdf.

44. Tessa Melvin, "Site of Artifacts Poses Quandary in Dobbs Ferry," *New York Times*, April 17, 1988, https://www.nytimes.com/1988/04/17/nyregion/site-of-artifacts-poses-quandary-in-dobbs-ferry.html; Hans Schaper, "Shell Middens in the Lower Hudson Valley," *The Bulletin* 98 (Spring 1989): 13–24, https://nysarchaeology.org/download/nysaa/bulletin/number_098.pdf; Kristin Clyne-Lehmann, "Indigenous Shell Middens of NYC," ArcGIS StoryMaps, December 20, 2022, https://storymaps.arcgis.com/stories/23768738db6d4e83b25dc2d9f6634f5e.

45. Jasper Danckaerts, *Journal of Jasper Danckaerts, 1679–1680*, ed. Bartlett Burleigh James and J. Franklin Jameson (New York: Charles Scribner's Sons, 1913), 54.

46. Adrienne Day and John Steele, "The Return of New York Harbor's Oysters," *Nautilus*, April 20, 2022, https://nautil.us/the-return-of-new-york-harbors-oysters-238466/;

"Oyster Reefs," Billion Oyster Project, accessed July 31, 2024, https://www.billionoyster project.org/reefs.

47. William K. Brooks, *The Oyster: A Popular Summary of a Scientific Study* (Baltimore: The Johns Hopkins Press, 1891), 12.

48. Pete Malinowski, "The Journey to One Billion Oysters with One Million New Yorkers," April 28, 2023, by Bailey-Matthews National Shell Museum and Aquarium, YouTube, 56 min., 50 sec., https://youtu.be/UwXwMbwqL-E?feature=shared.

49. "What We Do," New York Harbor School, accessed July 18, 2024, https://www. newyorkharborschool.org/what-we-do.

50. "Oyster Research Stations," Billion Oyster Project, accessed July 18, 2024, https:// www.billionoysterproject.org/ors.

51. Mark Kurlansky, *The Big Oyster: History on the Half Shell* (New York: Ballantine Books, 2006), 48–50.

5. Weathering

1. Jon Nordheimer, "Major Hurricane Threatens Middle of East Coast," *New York Times*, September 26, 1985, https://www.nytimes.com/1985/09/26/us/major-hurricane-threatens-middle-of-east-coast.html.

2. Lisa W. Foderaro, "Hurricane Filled New York Aquarium with Dangerous Substance: Water," *New York Times*, November 8, 2012, https://www.nytimes.com/2012/11/08/nyregion/hurricane-filled-new-york-aquarium-with-dangerous-substance-water.html.

3. Adriaen van der Donck, *A Description of New Netherland*, ed. Charles T. Gehring and William A. Starna, trans. Diederik W. Goedhuys (Lincoln: University of Nebraska Press, 2010), Kindle locations 278–81.

4. "Uncertain Ferry Traffic. Boats Irregular in Trips and Delayed by Huge Ice Fields," *New York Times*, March 14, 1888, https://timesmachine.nytimes.com/times machine/1888/03/14/103168845.html?pageNumber=2.

5. Ed Bacon, *Boat Basin BULLetin*, no. 9 (December 2009): 5, https://all-nyc-yachts. com/BOAT%20BASIN%20BULLetin%20-%20Issue%209.pdf.

6. NYCdata, "Disasters: New York City (NYC) Mid-Atlantic Nor'easter of 1992," Weissman Center for International Business, Baruch College, City University of New York, accessed July 18, 2024, https://www.baruch.cuny.edu/nycdata/disasters/noreaster-1992.html.

7. Ed Bacon, *Boat Basin BULLetin*, no. 7 (December 2008): 16–17, https://all-nyc-yachts.com/BOAT%20BASIN%20BULLetin%20-%20Issue%207.pdf.

8. Rick Spilman, "All Available Boats—Captain Michael Day's Radio Call on 9/11/01," *Old Salt Blog*, September 10, 2021, https://www.oldsaltblog.com/2021/09/all-available-boats-captain-michael-days-radio-call-on-9-11-01/.

9. "New York City, NY Weather History," Weather Underground, accessed July 12, 2024, https://www.wunderground.com/history/daily/us/ny/new-york-city/KLGA/date/2009-1-15.

10. "Scientists Determine Geese Involved in Hudson River Plane Crash Were Migratory," Smithsonian Institute, June 8, 2009, https://www.si.edu/newsdesk/releases/scientists-determine-geese-involved-hudson-river-plane-crash-were-migratory.

11. M. A. Farber, "79th St. Boat Basin, Called Fire Hazard, to Be Shut," *New York Times*, October 20, 1980, https://timesmachine.nytimes.com/timesmachine/1980/10/22/111302216. pdf?pdf_redirect=true&ip=0.

12. Author's personal papers.

13. Author's personal papers.

6. Goodbyes

1. Kim Velsey, "Twilight of the Liveaboards," *Curbed,* July 2, 2021, https://www.curbed.com/2021/07/twilight-of-the-liveaboards-the-79th-street-boat-basin.html.

2. Ben Yakas, "The 79th Street Boat Basin Redesign Is Making Everyone Feel Seasick," *Gothamist,* January 24, 2022, https://gothamist.com/arts-entertainment/79th-street-boat-basin-redesign-making-everyone-feel-seasick.

3. My emphasis. Manhattan Community Board 7, "06_June 18 '24_FB Proposed Resos," June 18, 2024, https://airtable.com/apppjjzIbJnWcCZta/shrEuacUFn82rYdYA/tbl 5KK4P74FGrNDai/viwUmh2KIo9GaGDHa/recLNvFQBBkUeSMNb.

Epilogue

1. "About CURB," Center for the Urban River at Beczak, accessed July 19, 2024, https://www.centerfortheurbanriver.org/about/.

2. "About," Hudson River Environmental Conditions Observing System, accessed July 19, 2024, https://hrecos.org/about/.

3. "About," NY Sun Works, accessed February 19, 2025, https://nysunworks.org/about/our-story/.

4. "Book a Group," Groundwork Hudson Valley, accessed July 19, 2024, https://www.groundworkhv.org/programs/sustainability-education/science-barge/science-barge-book-a-group/.

5. "Clearwater's Key to Common Hudson River Fishes," Hudson River Sloop Clearwater, Inc., last updated 2018, http://fishkey.clearwater.org.

6. "The Sailing Classroom," Hudson River Sloop Clearwater, updated 2025, https://www.clearwater.org/education/sailing-classroom/.

7. "Hudson River Field Station," Lamont-Doherty Earth Observatory, accessed July 19, 2014, https://lamont.columbia.edu/ldeo-hudson-river-field-station.

8. Margie Turrin, email message to the author, April 12, 2023.

9. Lamont-Doherty Earth Observatory, "Is the Hudson a River or an Estuary?: High School Version," Columbia University Earth Institute, accessed July 19, 2024, https://www.ldeo.columbia.edu/edu/k12/snapshotday/activities/2021/STEMHudsonRiver_HS.pdf, page 1.

10. "A Day in the Life of the Hudson Harbor," Hudson River Environmental Conditions Observing System, 2023, https://hrecos.org/a-day-in-the-life-of-the-hudson-harbor/.

11. NYSDEC, "Day in the Life of the Hudson & Harbor," April 27, 2023, YouTube, 3 min., 17 sec., https://youtu.be/BW90wiNYFW0?si=L8RX_E2REGoaFdMt.

12. Hudson River Estuary Program, "Hudson River Estuary Action Agenda 2021–2025," New York State Department of Environmental Conservation, accessed July 19, 2024, https://www.dec.ny.gov/docs/remediation_hudson_pdf/hreaa2021.pdf, page 18.

13. "Teaching About the Hudson River Estuary," New York State Department of Environmental Conservation, accessed February 20, 2025, https://dec.ny.gov/get-involved/education/teacher-information/teaching-hudson-river-estuary; "Hudson River Almanac," New York State Department of Environmental Conservation, accessed February 20, 2025, https://dec.ny.gov/nature/waterbodies/oceans-estuaries/hudson-river-estuary-program/hudson-river-almanac.

14. "Teachers," Billion Oyster Project, accessed July 19, 2024, https://www.billionoysterproject.org/educators.

15. "Oyster Research Stations," Billion Oyster Project, accessed July 18, 2024, https://www.billionoysterproject.org/ors.

BIBLIOGRAPHY

American Museum of Natural History. "Birding at the Museum: Frank Chapman and the Dioramas." December 20, 2013. YouTube. 4 min., 9 sec. https://youtu.be/qb6j72hPC7E?feature=shared.

Bacon, Ed. *Boat Basin BULLetin*, no. 7 (December 2008): 1–21. http://all-nyc-yachts.com/BOAT%20BASIN%20BULLetin%20-%20Issue%207.pdf.

Bacon, Ed. *Boat Basin BULLetin*, no. 9 (December 2009): 1–20. https://all-nyc-yachts.com/BOAT%20BASIN%20BULLetin%20-%20Issue%209.pdf

Baldwin, Jamie and Sönke Johnsen. "The Importance of Color in Mate Choice of the Blue Crab *Callinectes sapidus*." *Journal of Experimental Biology* 212, no. 22 (November 2009): 3762–68.

Barrymore Film Center. "A History of Film in Fort Lee, NJ." Accessed July 17, 2024. www.barrymorefilmcenter.com/history.

Berman, Bob. "What Are Spring Tides & Neap Tides?" *Almanac*. November 30, 2023. https://www.almanac.com/what-are-spring-tides-neap-tides.

Bill A3183. Assembly No. 3183, State of New Jersey, 216th Legislature. 2014. https://www.njleg.state.nj.us/bill-search/2014/A3183/bill-text?f=A3500&n=3183_I1.

Billion Oyster Project. "Oyster Reefs." Accessed July 31, 2024. https://www.billionoysterproject.org/reefs.

Billion Oyster Project. "Oyster Research Stations." Accessed July 18, 2024. https://www.billionoysterproject.org/ors.

Billion Oyster Project. "Teachers." Accessed July 19, 2024. https://www.billionoyster project.org/educators.

Binnewies, Robert O. *Palisades: The People's Park.* 2nd ed. New York: Fordham University Press, 2021.

Boyle, Robert H. *The Hudson River: A Natural and Unnatural History.* New York: W. W. Norton, 1979.

Broad, William J. "How the Ice Age Shaped New York." *New York Times,* June 5, 2018. https://www.nytimes.com/2018/06/05/science/how-the-ice-age-shaped-new-york.html.

Brooks, William K. *The Oyster: A Popular Summary of a Scientific Study.* Baltimore: The Johns Hopkins Press, 1891.

Caro, Robert A. *The Power Broker: Robert Moses and the Fall of New York.* New York: Alfred A. Knopf, 1974.

Carson, Rachel. *Silent Spring.* 40th anniversary ed. Boston: Houghton Mifflin, 2002.

Center for the Urban River at Beczak. "About CURB." Accessed July 19, 2024. https:// www.centerfortheurbanriver.org/about/.

Center for the Urban River at Beczak. "Hudson River Animal of the Month: Blue Crab." Accessed July 29, 2024. https://www.centerfortheurbanriver.org/news-events/ news/bluecrab-facts.html.

Charlé, Suzanne. "The Javits Center: Leading from the Rooftops." NYC Bird Alliance. Accessed July 31, 2024. https://nycbirdalliance.org/blog/the-javits-center-leading-from-the-rooftops.

Clyne-Lehmann, Kristin. "Indigenous Shell Middens of NYC." ArcGIS StoryMaps. December 20, 2022. https://storymaps.arcgis.com/stories/23768738db6d4e83b25d c2d9f6634f5e.

Conway, John. "Shad: The Founding Fish Returns." *New York Almanack,* May 13, 2014. https://www.newyorkalmanack.com/2014/05/shad-the-founding-fish-returns/.

Danckaerts, Jasper. *Journal of Jasper Danckaerts, 1679–1680.* Edited by Bartlett Burleigh James and J. Franklin Jameson. New York: Charles Scribner's Sons, 1913.

Danvers, E. L. "A Shanty Town Along the Hudson River." *I Love the Upper West Side.* Last modified April 4, 2023. ilovetheupperwestside.com/a-shanty-town-along-the-hudson-river/#google_vignette.

Davis, E. Emory, and Eric Nelsen. *New Jersey's Palisades Interstate Park.* Charleston, SC: Arcadia Library Editions, 2007.

Day, Adrienne, and John Steele. "The Return of New York Harbor's Oysters." *Nautilus,* April 20, 2022. https://nautil.us/the-return-of-new-york-harbors-oysters-238466/.

Day, Leslie. *Field Guide to the Natural World of New York City.* Baltimore: Johns Hopkins University Press, 2007.

Day, Leslie. *Field Guide to the Neighborhood Birds of New York City.* Baltimore: Johns Hopkins University Press, 2015.

Dineen, Robert J., and William B. Rogers. "Sedimentary Environments in Glacial Lake Albany in the Albany Section of the Hudson-Champlain Lowlands." Paper in the guidebook for the Joint Annual Meeting of the New York State Geological Association 51st Annual Meeting and the New England Intercollegiate Geological Conference 71st Meeting, Troy, NY, October 5–7, 1979: 87–199. https://www.nysga-online.

org/wp-content/uploads/2019/06/NYSGA-1979-A3-Sedimentary-Environments-In-Glacial-Lake-Albany-In-The-Albany-Section-Of-The-Hudson-Champlain-Low lands.pdf.

Donck, Adriaen van der. *A Description of New Netherland*. Edited by Charles T. Gehring and William A. Starna. Translated by Diederik W. Goedhuys. Lincoln: University of Nebraska Press, 2010. Kindle.

Dwyer, Jim. "LG to Reduce Height of Headquarters, Preserving Palisades Horizon." *New York Times*, June 23, 2015. www.nytimes.com/2015/06/24/nyregion/lg-to-reduce-height-of-headquarters-preserving-palisades-horizon.html.

Eakin, Wes, Gregg Kenney, and ElizaBeth Streifeneder. "Recovery Plan for Hudson River American Shad." New York State Department of Environmental Conservation, Division of Marine Resources. March 2023. https://extapps.dec.ny.gov/docs/fish_marine_pdf/hudsonshadplan.pdf.

The Elisabeth Morrow School. "Where We Started." Accessed July 17, 2024. https://elisabethmorrow.org/block-slider/the-history-of-ems/.

Farber, M. A. "79th St. Boat Basin, Called Fire Hazard, to Be Shut." *New York Times*, October 20, 1980. https://timesmachine.nytimes.com/timesmachine/1980/10/22/111302216.pdf?pdf_redirect=true&ip=0.

Foderaro, Lisa W. "Hurricane Filled New York Aquarium with Dangerous Substance: Water." *New York Times*, November 8, 2012. https://www.nytimes.com/2012/11/08/nyregion/hurricane-filled-new-york-aquarium-with-dangerous-substance-water.html.

FortTryon Park Trust. "The Palisades." Accessed July 17, 2024. https://www.forttryonparktrust.org/the-palisades/.

Gavan, Peggy. "1933: Herbert Hoover and Andy Mellon, the Pet Pigs of Camp Thomas Paine." *The Hatching Cat of Gotham: True and Unusual Animal Tales of Old New York*, January 4, 2021. https://hatchingcatnyc.com/2021/01/04/pet-pigs-camp-thomas-paine/.

Greenhouse, Linda. "Pollution Accusations Against G.M. Dismay North Tarrytown." *New York Times*, January 12, 1971. https://www.nytimes.com/1971/01/12/archives/pollution-accusations-against-gm-dismay-north-tarrytown.html.

Groundwork Hudson Valley. "Book a Group." Accessed July 19. 2024. https://www.groundworkhv.org/programs/sustainability-education/science-barge/science-barge-book-a-group/.

Haffner, Jeanne. "The Palisades in Peril: Meet the Forgotten Women Who Fought to Save the Great Cliffs of the Hudson River." The New-York Historical. April 30, 2019. https://www.nyhistory.org/blogs/palisades-peril-forgotten-women-saved.

Heller, Ruth. *A Sea Within a Sea: Secrets of the Sargasso*. New York: Grosset & Dunlap, 2000.

Holzer, Judith, Kathleen Modrowski, Catherine Walter, and Hans Schaper. *Wickers Creek Archaeological Site: What You Should Know*. 2nd ed. Dobbs Ferry, NY: The Friends of Wickers Creek Archaeological Site, 2005. http://75.103.101.60/documents/curriculum_speigelman_Friends_of_Wickers_Creek_Analysis.pdf.

Hudson, Edward. "City's Largest Sewage Plant Is Going upon the Hudson." *New York Times*, September 2, 1972, https://timesmachine.nytimes.com/timesmachine/1972/09/02/81957590.pdf?pdf_redirect=true&ip=0.

Hudson River Environmental Conditions Observing System. "About." Accessed July 19, 2024. https://hrecos.org/about/.

Hudson River Environmental Conditions Observing System. "A Day in the Life of the Hudson Harbor." 2023. https://hrecos.org/a-day-in-the-life-of-the-hudson-harbor/.

Hudson River Estuary Program. "Growing Up As a Striped Bass." New York State Department of Environmental Conservation. Accessed July 19, 2024. https://extapps. dec.ny.gov/docs/remediation_hudson_pdf/hrlpk3sbass.pdf.

Hudson River Estuary Program. "Hudson River Estuary Action Agenda 2021–2025." New York State Department of Environmental Conservation. Accessed July 19, 2024. https://www.dec.ny.gov/docs/remediation_hudson_pdf/hreaa2021.pdf.

Hudson River Sloop Clearwater, Inc. "Clearwater's Key to Common Hudson River Fishes." Last updated 2018. http://fishkey.clearwater.org.

Hudson River Sloop Clearwater. "The Sailing Classroom." Updated 2025. https://www. clearwater.org/education/sailing-classroom/.

Hudson River Sloop Clearwater. "The Sloop." Accessed July 29, 2024. https://www. clearwater.org/the-sloop/.

Hutcheson, Hilary. "Managing Menhaden: The Most Important Fish in the Sea." *Fly Fisherman*, May 25, 2021. https://www.flyfisherman.com/editorial/menhaden-most-important-fish-in-sea/392897.

Kang, Tricia. "What Lies Beneath: A History of Collect Pond." Tenement Museum. Accessed July 12, 2024. https://www.tenement.org/blog/what-lies-beneath-a-history-of-collect-pond/.

Kiernan, John. *Natural History of New York City*. New York: Houghton Mifflin, 1959.

Knowles, Elizabeth, ed. *The Oxford Dictionary of Phrase and Fable*. 2nd ed. Oxford: Oxford University Press, 2005.

Kurlansky, Mark. *The Big Oyster: History on the Half Shell*. New York: Ballantine Books, 2006.

Lamont-Doherty Earth Observatory. "Hudson River Field Station." Accessed July 19, 2024. https://lamont.columbia.edu/ldeo-hudson-river-field-station.

Lamont-Doherty Earth Observatory. "Is the Hudson a River or an Estuary?: High School Version." Columbia University Earth Institute. Accessed July 19, 2024. https://www. ldeo.columbia.edu/edu/k12/snapshotday/activities/2021/STEMHudsonRiver_HS.pdf.

Langlois, Richard J. "The Hudson River Sloop Clearwater: Sailing to Save the River." Hudson River Valley Institute. Accessed February 2, 2025. https://www. hudsonrivervalley.org/sloop-clearwater#:~:text=Many%20of%20Clearwater's%20 passengers%20are,sloop!"%20said%20Captain%20Flynn.

Levine, David. "The Flood That Created the Hudson Valley." *Times Union*, July 16, 2023. https://www.timesunion.com/hudsonvalley/article/flood-ice-age-glacial-lake-iroquois-18199700.php.

Levine, Lucie. "Looking Back at the Depression-Era Shanty Towns in New York City Parks." 6sqft. February 26, 2020. https://www.6sqft.com/looking-back-at-the-depression-era-shanty-towns-in-new-york-city-parks/.

Lund, Ann. "Undercliff Cemetery/Whack Me Jug Grave, Englewood Cliffs NY." *Free-HiddenWorld (Exploring Local NY/NJ History)*, June 28, 2020. freehiddenworld. wordpress.com/2020/06/28/undercliff-cemetery-whack-me-jug-grave.

Malinowski, Pete. "The Journey to One Billion Oysters with One Million New Yorkers." April 28, 2023, by Bailey-Matthews National Shell Museum and Aquarium. YouTube, 56 min., 50 sec. https://youtu.be/UwXwMbwqL-E?feature=shared.

Manhattan Community Board 7. "06_June 18 '24_FB Proposed Resos." Accessed February 18, 2025. https://airtable.com/apppjjzIbJnWcCZta/shrEuacUFn82rYdYA/tbl5KK4P74FGrNDai/viwUmh2KIo9GaGDHa/recLNvFQBBkUeSMNb.

McCully, Betsy. "Ice Age History: How Glaciers Shaped New York." New York Nature. Updated August 25, 2023. https://www.newyorknature.us/ice-age-new-york/.

Melvin, Tessa. "Site of Artifacts Poses Quandary in Dobbs Ferry." *New York Times*, April 17, 1988. https://www.nytimes.com/1988/04/17/nyregion/site-of-artifacts-poses-quandary-in-dobbs-ferry.html.

Milman, Oliver. "'They Are Amazed': New York City Sees Extraordinary Leap in Whale Sightings." *The Guardian*, June 3, 2019. https://www.theguardian.com/us-news/2019/jun/03/new-york-city-whale-sightings-increase.

Morison, Samuel Eliot. "The Sea in Literature." *The Atlantic*, September 1, 1955. https://www.theatlantic.com/magazine/archive/1955/09/the-sea-in-literature/641300/#.

The Nanticoke Lenni-Lenape: An American Indian Tribe. "Our Tribal History . . ." Accessed July 17, 2024. https://nanticoke-lenape.info/history.htm#:~:text=We%20called%20ourselves%20%22Lenni%2DLenape.

National Audubon Society. "History of the Christmas Bird Count." Accessed July 18, 2024. https://www.audubon.org/community-science/christmas-bird-count/history-christmas-bird-count.

National Ocean Service. "What is the Sargasso Sea?" Accessed July 29, 2024. https://oceanservice.noaa.gov/facts/sargassosea.html.

National Park Service. "Yonkers, New York." Accessed July 17, 2024. https://www.nps.gov/articles/000/yonkers-new-york.htm.

The Nature Conservancy. "The Return of the Most Important Fish in the Sea." February 12, 2020. https://www.nature.org/en-us/about-us/where-we-work/united-states/new-york/stories-in-new-york/menhaden-whales-return-new-york/.

New Netherland Institute. "Early Descriptions of New Netherland." Accessed February 2, 2025. https://www.newnetherlandinstitute.org/history-and-heritage/additional-resources/dutch-treats/early-impressions-of-new-netherland.

New York City Department of Environmental Protection. "New York City's Wastewater Treatment System." Accessed July 29, 2024. https://semspub.epa.gov/work/02/206372.pdf.

New York City Department of Parks and Recreation. "Minetta Green." Accessed July 12, 2024. https://www.nycgovparks.org/parks/minetta-green/history.

New York Harbor School. "What We Do." Accessed July 18, 2024. https://www.newyorkharborschool.org/what-we-do.

New-York Historical Society. "Hudson Highlands: Part 1." Accessed July 29, 2024. https://hudsonrising.nyhistory.org/hudson-highlands-part-1/.

The New York Preservation Archive Project. "Andrew Haswell Green." Accessed July 23, 2024. www.nypap.org/preservation-history/andrew-haswell-green/.

New York State Department of Environmental Conservation. "Atlantic Sturgeon." Accessed July 31, 2024. https://dec.ny.gov/nature/animals-fish-plants/hudson-delaware-marine-fisheries/atlantic-sturgeon.

New York State Department of Environmental Conservation. "Hudson River Almanac." Accessed February 20, 2025. https://dec.ny.gov/nature/waterbodies/oceans-estuaries/hudson-river-estuary-program/hudson-river-almanac.

New York State Department of Environmental Conservation. "Striped Bass." Accessed July 29, 2024. https://dec.ny.gov/nature/animals-fish-plants/hudson-delaware-marine-fisheries/striped-bass.

New York State Department of Environmental Conservation. "Teaching About the Hudson River Estuary." Accessed February 20, 2025. https://dec.ny.gov/get-involved/education/teacher-information/teaching-hudson-river-estuary.

New York State Department of Health. "Hudson River Fish Advisory Outreach Project." Accessed July 29, 2024. https://www.health.ny.gov/environmental/outdoors/fish/hudson_river/advisory_outreach_project/.

NOAA (National Oceanic and Atmospheric Administration) Fisheries. "Atlantic Sturgeon." Accessed July 31, 2024. https://www.fisheries.noaa.gov/species/atlantic-sturgeon.

NOAA Fisheries. "Fishing Gear: Purse Seines." Accessed July 29, 2024. https://www.fisheries.noaa.gov/national/bycatch/fishing-gear-purse-seines.

Nordheimer, Jon. "Major Hurricane Threatens Middle of East Coast." *New York Times*, September 26, 1985. https://www.nytimes.com/1985/09/26/us/major-hurricane-threatens-middle-of-east-coast.html.

NYCdata. "Disasters: New York City (NYC) Mid-Atlantic Nor'easter of 1992." Weissman Center for International Business, Baruch College, City University of New York. Accessed July 18, 2024. https://www.baruch.cuny.edu/nycdata/disasters/noreaster-1992.html.

NYC Parks. "Cadman Plaza Park." Accessed July 31, 2024. https://www.nycgovparks.org/parks/cadman-plaza-park-and-brooklyn-war-memorial/highlights/12535.

NYSDEC. "Day in the Life of the Hudson & Harbor." April 27, 2023. YouTube. 3 min., 17 sec. https://youtu.be/BW90wiNYFW0?si=L8RX_E2REGoaFdMt.

NY Sun Works. "About." Accessed February 19, 2025. https://nysunworks.org/about/our-story/.

Oceana. "Lion's Mane Jellyfish." Accessed July 31, 2024. https://oceana.org/marine-life/lions-mane-jellyfish/.

Official Web Site of the Delaware Tribe of Indians. "Lenape Fishing." June 27, 2013. https://delawaretribe.org/blog/2013/06/27/lenape-fishing/.

Olson, Danielle. "The Origin of Eels." Smithsonian Ocean. December 2022. https://ocean.si.edu/ocean-life/fish/origin-eels.

Palisades Interstate Park Commission. "Exploring Nature at the Palisades Interstate Park in New Jersey." Accessed July 17, 2024. www.njpalisades.org/nature.html.

Passe, Angèle Sancho. *Is Everybody Ready for Kindergarten?: A Toolkit for Preparing Children and Families*. St. Paul, MN: Redleaf Press, 2010.

Ripley, J. L. "Differential Parental Nutrient Allocation in Two Congeneric Pipefish Species (Syngnathidae: *Syngnathus* Spp.)." *Journal of Experimental Biology* 209, no. 6 (March 15, 2006): 1112–21. https://doi.org/10.1242/jeb.02119.

Riverkeeper. "The First People of the River." Accessed July 29, 2024. https://www.riverkeeper.org/hudson-river/hudson-river-journey/the-first-people-of-the-river/.

Sanderson, Eric. "Recreating Mannahatta." The Welikia Project. Accessed July 29, 2024. https://welikia.org/science/recreating-mannahatta/.

Sanderson, Eric W., and Markley Boyer. *Mannahatta: A Natural History of New York City*. New York: Abrams, 2009.

Schaper, Hans. "Shell Middens in the Lower Hudson Valley." *The Bulletin* 98 (Spring 1989): 13–24. https://nysarchaeology.org/download/nysaa/bulletin/number_098.pdf.

Schlichter, Tom. "Governor Cuomo Signs Bill to Protect Menhaden." *Outdoor Tom*, April 18, 2019. http://outdoortom.com/2019/04/5488/.

Schuberth, Christopher J. *The Geology of New York City and Environs*. Garden City, NY: The Natural History Press, 1968.

Schweber, Nate, and Sharon Otterman. "A Painfully Early Arrival for a Summer Nuisance." *New York Times*, July 22, 2008. https://www.nytimes.com/2008/07/22/nyregion/22jellyfish.html.

Smithsonian Institute. "Scientists Determine Geese Involved in Hudson River Plane Crash Were Migratory." June 8, 2009. https://www.si.edu/newsdesk/releases/scientists-determine-geese-involved-hudson-river-plane-crash-were-migratory.

Sparling, Reed. "The Shad Are Running—But for How Much Longer?" Scenic Hudson. Accessed July 31, 2024. https://www.scenichudson.org/viewfinder/the-shad-are-running-but-for-how-much-longer/.

Spilman, Rick. "All Available Boats—Captain Michael Day's Radio Call on 9/11/01." *Old Salt Blog*, September 10, 2021. https://www.oldsaltblog.com/2021/09/all-available-boats-captain-michael-days-radio-call-on-9-11-01/.

"Squatters Must Leave. Moses Orders Camp Thomas Paine on Hudson Vacated by May 1." *New York Times*, April 18, 1934. timesmachine.nytimes.com/timesmachine/1934/04/18/97142604.html?pageNumber=7.

Stanne, Stephen P., Roger G. Panetta, Brian E. Forist. *The Hudson: An Illustrated Guide to the Living River*. New Brunswick, NJ: Rutgers University Press, 1996.

Stern, Robert A. M., Gregory Gilmartin, and Thomas Mellins. *New York 1930: Architecture and Urbanism Between the Two World Wars*. New York: Rizzoli, 1987.

Taft, Dave. "Striped Bass of the Hudson." *New York Times*, October 14, 2016. https://www.nytimes.com/2016/10/16/nyregion/striped-bass-of-the-hudson.html.

Terres, John K. *The Audubon Society Encyclopedia of North American Birds*. Avenel, NJ: Wings Books, 1996.

Thorne, John. "Henry Hudson and the Half Moon, 1609." Gotham History. May 12, 2015. https://gothamhistory.com/2015/05/12/henry-hudson-and-the-half-moon-1609/.

"Uncertain Ferry Traffic. Boats Irregular in Trips and Delayed by Huge Ice Fields." *New York Times*, March 14, 1888. https://timesmachine.nytimes.com/timesmachine/1888/03/14/103168845.html?pageNumber=2.

United States Environmental Protection Agency. "History of the Clean Water Act." Last updated June 12, 2024. https://www.epa.gov/laws-regulations/history-clean-water-act.

US Fish and Wildlife Service. "American Eel." Accessed July 29, 2024. https://www.fws.gov/species/american-eel-anguilla-rostrata.

Velsey, Kim. "Twilight of the Liveaboards." *Curbed*, July 2, 2021. https://www.curbed.com/2021/07/twilight-of-the-liveaboards-the-79th-street-boat-basin.html.

Vilacoba, Karl. "Ocean Story #8: In Gotham City, a Dark Sight Rises." Mid-Atlantic Ocean Data Portal. Accessed July 17, 2024. https://portal.midatlanticocean.org/ocean-stories/gotham-whale-new-york-humpbacks/.

Virginia Institute of Marine Science. "Swimming Blue Crab." May 10, 2017. YouTube. 36 sec. https://youtu.be/tzjKduvXz5Y?feature=shared.

Warner, William W. *Beautiful Swimmers*. New York: Little, Brown, 1994.

Wave Hill. "19th Century and the Perkins Legacy." Accessed July 18, 2024. https://www.wavehill.org/discover/our-mission-history/19th-century-and-the-perkins-legacy.

Weather Underground. "New York City, NY Weather History." Accessed July 12, 2024. https://www.wunderground.com/history/daily/us/ny/new-york-city/KLGA/date/2009-1-15.

Weise, Arthur James. *The Discoveries of America to the Year 1525*. New York: G. P. Putnam's Sons, 1884. https://www.gutenberg.org/cache/epub/67766/pg67766-images.html#CHAPTER_IX.

Winston, Tod. *New York City Audubon's Harbor Herons Project: 2021 Nesting Survey Report*. New York: New York City Audubon, 2021. https://www.hudsonriver.org/wp-content/uploads/2022/06/2021_HH_Interim_Survey_Report.pdf.

Yakas, Ben. "The 79th Street Boat Basin Redesign Is Making Everyone Feel Seasick." *Gothamist*, January 24, 2022. https://gothamist.com/arts-entertainment/79th-street-boat-basin-redesign-making-everyone-feel-seasick.

Zimmer, Carl. "How Flounder Wound Up with an Epic Side-Eye." *New York Times*, June 21, 2024. https://www.nytimes.com/2024/06/21/science/flounder-flatfish-evolution.html.

INDEX

Acipenser brevirostrum, shortnose
  sturgeon, 76, 78*fig*
Acipenser oxyrinchus, Atlantic sturgeon,
  76–79, 95*fig*
algae, 51, 63, 67, 70, 72, 132
Alosa sapidissima, American shad, 75–76
Amelanchier canadensis, shadblow tree, 76
American eel, 70–72, 81, 119*fig*
American Museum of Natural History, 8,
  18, 43, 82–83, 92
American Scenic and Historic
  Preservation Society, 6, 18
Ammann, Othmar, and George
  Washington Bridge, 4
Anguila rostrata, American eel, 70–72,
  81, 119*fig*
Annunziato, Marisa, (Lamont-Doherty
  Earth Observatory), 132
Atlantic menhaden, mossbunker, iii*fig*,
  60, 62–65

Atlantic States Marine Fisheries
  Commission, 64
Audubon, John James, 55
  Minniesland, 55
Audobon, Victor, 55
Auletta, Gina, 24
Aurelia aurita, moon jelly, 13*fig*, 79

Bacon, Ed, 34, 36, 99–100, 99*fig*, 108–9,
  112–13, 118
bass, striped, 53, 55, 60, 62–64, 73–75,
  127*fig*, 129
bathing beaches, Hudson River, 9, 9*fig*
Berlin, Meg, 28, 35
Berney, Lonn, 116
Billion Oyster Project, 92–94, 135
Bloomberg, Michael, 96, 108*fig*, 109
Bloomer's Beach, 8–9, 9*fig*
Bloomgarden, Josh, 28–29, 29*fig*
Bowser, Chris, 133

Boyle, Robert, 56

brackish water, 52

Breslov, Lisa, 92–93

Brevoortia patronus, Atlantic menhaden, iii*fig*, 60, 62–65

Brewer, Gale, 121–22

Brooklyn College, 27, 46, 106, 111

Buhrer, Raquel and Werner, 35, 44, 95, 102, 103*fig*, 117*fig*

Calhoun School, 45, 47*fig*, 105–6, 120

Callinectes sapidus, blue crab, 43*fig*, 72–73

Camp Thomas Paine, Hooverville on Hudson River, 19–20

Caplow, Ted, NY Sun Works, 129

Capozzi, Michele, 35–37

caprellids, skeleton shrimp, 63–64

cardinal, northern, 44–45, 44*fig*

Caro, Robert, *The Power Broker*, 18–19

Carpenter Brothers' Quarry, 6*fig*, 7

Carson, Rachel, *Silent Spring*, 84

catch limits, menhaden, 64

Center for the Urban River (CURB), 127–29, 128*fig*

chelipeds, 72

chromatophores, 69–70

Clean Water Act (1972), 57, 60, 62

Clearwater, Hudson River Sloop, 50, 58–60, 59*fig*, 75, 126*fig*, 131, 131*fig*

Clegg, Jane, 35

cliffhanger (term), 8

cohesion, of water molecules, 32

Columbia University, 47, 59, 132–33

Columbus, Christopher, 53

comb jellies, 67–68

cormorants, double-crested, 80–82, 80*fig*

COVID-19, 119–20

crabs, blue, 43*fig*, 62, 72–73, 94, 129

Ctenophores, 67–68

Cuomo, Andrew, 64

currents, 15–16, 51, 70

Cyanea capillata, lion's mane jellyfish, 61*fig*, 79–80

Day, Leslie, photographs of, v*fig*, 3*fig*, 28*fig*, 34*fig*, 42*fig*, 47*fig*, 49*figs*, 62*fig*, 108*fig*, 117*fig*, 125*fig*

Day, Michael, Lt. US Coast Guard and 9/11, 112

Day in the Life of the Hudson event, 59, 131, 131*fig*, 133–34

DDT, 83–84, 86

decapods, 72

Description of New Netherland, A (van der Donck), 54, 98

Di Bagno, Simone, 35–37, 124

diabase, Palisades, 5–6, 10

DiPaolo, Germaine, 48, 110

Dove, Carla, Smithsonian National Museum of Natural History, 114

ducks, mallard, 38–39, 40*fig*, 114, 122

Duke (dog), 7

eagles, bald, 84–86, 85*fig*

ebb tide, 15

eels, American, 70–72, 81

Elisabeth Morrow School, The, 47–48, 49*fig*, 61, 131*fig*

Ellis Island, Little Oyster Island, 91

Endangered Species Act, 86

Englewood Boat Basin, 8

Englewood Cliffs, New Jersey, 1–2, 10–11

Environmental Protection Agency (EPA), 57

estuaries, 17, 92, 133

Falco peregrinus, peregrine falcon, 82–84, 84*fig*

Field Guide to the Neighborhood Birds of New York City (Day), 82

Fisher, Murray, 93

Fisherman's Village, 8

Fitzpatrick, Joe, 116

flatfish, 69–70

flood tide, 15–16, 99

Fort Lee, New Jersey, as film capital, 8

freezing point of water, 97–98

geese, Canada, 39, 40*fig*, 41, 41*fig*, 113–15
George Washington Bridge, 4–5, 7, 47, 55–56
Gershenhorn, Ira, 93–94
gills/gill flaps, 63, 70, 76–77
Glowka, Art, 56
Grand Parade of Sailing Ships, 34, 34*fig*
Great Oyster Island, Liberty Island, 91
Green, Andrew Haswell, 6, 18
gribbles, crustaceans, 121
Groundwork Hudson Valley, 130
gulls, black-backed, herring, and ring-billed, 88–90, 88*fig*

Haliaeetus leucocephalus, bald eagle, 84–86, 85*fig*
Hayama, Kazumi, 28
Heart Mountain Relocation Center, 24, 24*fig*, 25, 25*fig*, 26*figs*, 27*fig*
heating, on boats, 104–5
Henry Hudson Parkway, 20, 106, 113
Henry the duck, 39, 40*fig*
heron, black-crowned night, 87–88
hogchokers, 62, 69–70
Hooverville, on the Hudson, 19–20
Horenstein, Sidney, 8
Hudson, Henry, 53, 91
Hudson, The: An Illustrated Guide to the Living River, (Stanne et al.), 50
Hudson Harbor Preservation Association, 35, 116
Hudson Lab School, 125, 127–29, 128*fig*
Hudson Rising exhibition, New-York Historical Society, 59*fig*, 75
Hudson River Almanac (Lake), 61, 134
Hudson River, geologic history, 51–52
Hudson River Environmental Conditions Observing System (HRECOS), 129
Hudson River Estuary Program (HREP), 50, 59, 133, 134
Hudson River Fish Advisory Outreach Project, 58
Hudson River Fishermen's Association (HRFA), 56–58, 60, 61, 75

Hudson River Foundation, 61, 75
Hudson River, The (Boyle), 56
humpback whales, 63, 65*fig*
hurricanes, 96–97, 121
Hurtwing (Canada goose), 39, 40*fig*, 113
Hynes, Doug, 35

ice and ice floes, 97–100, 102, 103*figs*, 104
    bald eagles on, 85
    seals on, 65, 66*fig*

Jamaica Bay Wildlife Refuge, 82, 88
Japanese internment camps, and Nishiura family, 24–26, 26*figs*, 27*fig*
jellyfish, moon and lion's mane, 13*fig*, 61*fig*, 79–80
Jordan, Paul, 99, 99*fig*
Juet, Robert, 53

Kane, Cindy, 35, 42, 42*fig*
Katzman, Doron, 42*fig*, 103*fig*
Kieran, John, *A Natural History of New York City*, 85

Lake, Tom, 61, 69, 134
lakes, glacial, Albany, Hudson, and Iroquois, 51–52
Lamont-Doherty Earth Observatory (LDEO), 59, 132–33, 132*fig*
Larus delawarensis, ring-billed gull, 88–89, 88*fig*
Larus marinus, great black-backed gull, 89
Larus smithsonianus, herring gull, 89–90
Laurentide Ice Sheet, 51, 52
Lenni-Lenape, 1, 52–56, 76, 90–91
Letts, Christopher, 61, 62*fig*, 69–70, 127
Liberty Island, Great Oyster Island, 91
Lispenard Creek, 54–55
Little Oyster Island, Ellis Island, 91
Lowry, David, 48, 110

mal de débarquement syndrome, 16
Malinowski, Peter, 92–93

Mandala, houseboat, 13–15, 80, 100
Manhattan, 2–5, 7–10, 17, 20, 36,
    51–55, 57, 89–90, 92, 96, 98, 106,
    110–13, 114, 121–23
Manhattan Community Board, 7,
    122–24
Mannahatta, 52–57
*Mannahatta: A Natural History of New
    York City,* (Sanderson), 17
Marra, Pete, Smithsonian Migratory Bird
    Center, 114–15
Maya (dog), 95, 100
Megaptera novaeangliae, humpback
    whale, 65*fig*
menhaden, Atlantic, 60, 62–63, 64–65
middens, oyster, 90
Milne, Carolyn and George, 111
Minetta Brook, 54
"Miracle on the Hudson," 113–15
Molly (dog), 102, 117*fig*
moon, and tides, 15, 36, 50, 124
Morgan, J. P., 6–7
Morone saxatilis, striped bass, 73–75, 127*fig*
Moses, Robert, 18–20
mossbunker, menhaden, 60, 62–65
mudsnails, eastern, 51
Murat, Annick, 28*fig*
Murat, Didier, 103*fig*

Narrows, The, 51–52
National Historic and Natural Landmark
    designations, Hudson River, 10
National Museum of Natural History,
    Smithsonian, 114
National Oceanic and Atmospheric
    Administration (NOAA), 64
National Register of Historic Places, 60
Natural Resources Defense Council,
    10, 75
neap tides, 50
nematocysts, of jellyfish, 79
Nessim (cat), 14–15, 30, 101
New Jersey Conservation Foundation, 10
New Jersey State Federation of Women's
    Clubs, 6–7, 10

New York Central Railroad, 17–19
New York City Audubon, 82
New York City Department of Parks and
    Recreation, 115–18, 121–22
New York City Economic Development
    Corporation, 122
New York City Landmarks Preservation
    Commission, 21
New York Harbor Act (1888), 56
New York State Department of
    Environmental Conservation, 50,
    59, 61, 74, 76, 129, 133–34
New York State Department of Health, 58
New York-New Jersey Trail Conference, 10
New-York Historical Society, 59*fig*, 75
Nicolau, Lisa, 110
Nin, Anaïs, *Collages,* 14
9/11 (September 11, 2001), 110–13
Nishiura, Aya, 24, 94, 127, 128*fig*
Nishiura, Jim, 22–25, 27–29, 27*fig*,
    30*fig*, 31, 39, 89, 95, 97, 100–102,
    104–8, 111, 116, 119–20
Nishiura, Jonah, 24, 30*fig*, 31, 32, 35,
    95–96, 105–6, 111, 116, 117*fig*,
    127–28
Nishiura family, 23–27, 23*fig*, 25*fig*,
    26*fig*, 27*fig*
nitrogen, in Hudson River, 92
nor'easters, 41, 96, 105–7, 107*fig*, 121
North River Sewage Treatment Plant,
    60, 62
Nycticorax nycticorax, black-crowned
    night heron, 87–88

Olmsted, Frederick Law, and Riverside
    Park, 18
osprey, 63, 84–87, 87*fig*
oxygen, and dissolved oxygen levels, 32,
    59, 60, 70, 92, 134
oysters, American, 53, 90–92, 93–94,
    134–35, 135*fig*

Palisades, 1–2, 4–11, 6*fig*, 9*fig*, 18, 47,
    52, 55, 61, 71, 83, 125, 126*fig*
Palisades Interstate Park, 7, 9*fig*, 10, 71

Palisades Interstate Park Commission, 5, 7, 75, 138
Palisades Interstate Parkway, 5, 47–48
pandemic, COVID-19 119–20
Pandion haliaetus, osprey, 86, 87*fig*
Pangaea, breaking up and formation of Palisades, 5
Parsons, Samuel, Jr., 18
Penn Central Railroad, 56, 60
peregrine falcon, 82–84, 84*fig*
Perkins, George, 6–7
Phalacrocorax auritus, double-crested cormorant, 80–82, 80*fig*
Phoca vitulina, harbor seal, 65–67, 66*figs*
phytoplankton, 51, 63, 132–34
Pickletown, 8
pipefish, northern, 1*fig*, 62, 68–69
Pirone, Dominick, Hudson River Fisherman's Association, 58
pollution, 9–10, 56–58, 60, 64, 92
polychlorinated biphenyls (PCBs), in Hudson River, 57–58, 60
Porter, Troy, 102, 103*fig*
Purrington, Tom, 113
purse seine nets, 64

quarrying, of Palisades, 5–8, 6*fig*

Refuse Act (1899), 56
Riepe, Don, 81
Riverkeeper, 57, 76
Rivers and Harbors Act (1888), 56
Riverside Drive, 18, 83
Riverside Park, 4, 12, 16, 18–21, 35, 37, 45, 100, 111, 122
Robbins, Alan, 117*fig*
Rockefeller, John D., Jr., 7
Rockefeller, John D., Sr., 6–7
Rockefeller, Laurance, Jr., 10–11
Roosevelt, Franklin D., 24
Roosevelt, Teddy, 7
Rotunda, 79th Street, 20–21, 21*fig*, 123

Sadie (dog), 48, 49*fig*, 113
San Jose Buddhist Church Betsuin, 23, 23*fig*

Sanderson, Eric, *Mannahatta: A Natural History of New York City*, 17, 55
Sanibel, houseboat, 97, 105, 107–8
Sarah Lawrence College, and Center for the Urban River (CURB), 128–29, 128*fig*
Sargasso Sea, and eels, 70–72
Scenic Hudson Preservation Conference, 10, 75
Schuster, Eleanor, 110
Schwab, Charles, 19–20
Science Barge, 129–30, 130*fig*
seahorses, and pipefish, 68–69
seals, harbor, 65, 66*fig*, 67
Seeger, Pete, 58, 59*fig*, 60
seine nets/seining, 59, 61–62, 62*fig*, 64, 69, 128, 132, 133
79th Street Boat Basin
    closing and redesign of, 120–24
    gardens, 27–29, 28*fig*, 29*fig*, 45–46
    holidays, 33–35, 34*fig*
    ice floes, 98–100, 99*fig*, 102–4, 103*figs*
    ice skating, 99*fig*
    infrastructure, failing, 121
    moving to, 4, 13–15
    Robert Moses, 20
    storms, 41–42, 95–107, 107*fig*
    tides, 15, 50–51, 57, 98, 106, 121
    See also individual residents
sewage, in the Hudson, 57, 60, 62, 91
shad, American, 53, 55, 75–76
Shorakapok, 90
Shorter, Kenneth, Judge, 116, 118
sickness of disembarkation, 16
Silent Spring (Carson), 84
sinking, 35, 107–9, 121
skeleton shrimp, caprellids, 63
slack tides, 15
Smith, Gregory, dockmaster, 78, 111
Smithsonian Institution, 25
Smithsonian Migratory Bird Center, 114–15
Smoke, Leslee, 35
Smoke, Trudy, 117*fig*, 120

Spot (dog), 95, 100–101
spring tides, 50
stable isotope analysis, of bird strikes,
    115
Stephens, Ray, 35, 100–101, 117*fig*
Stern, Henry, 116, 121
Storm King Power Plant, and striped
    bass, 75
sturgeon, Atlantic and shortnose, 53,
    76–79, 78*fig*, 90, 95*fig*
sukkahs, on houseboats, 33
Sullenberger, Chesley "Sully," 114
swans, mute, 35, 39, 41–42, 42*fig*, 106
Sygnathus fuscus, northern pipefish, 1*fig*,
    68–69

tides, on Hudson River, 15–16, 50–51
Tranquility, houseboat, 105*fig*
Trinectes maculatus, hogchoker,
    69–70
Tritia obsoleta, eastern mudsnail, 51
turbidity, measuring, 134
Turrin, Margie, 132–33

Undercliff, village and cemetery, 8
uropygial glands, of birds, 81

van der Donck, Adriaen, 53–54, 98
Vaux, Calvert, and Riverside Park, 18
Verrazzano, Giovanni da, 53
Voorhees, Foster McGowan, 7

Wachtel, Lena and Julian (grandparents), 4
water
    cohesion, 32

freezing point of, 97–98
molecular structure of, 31–32
watersheds, 133–34
Wave Hill estate, and Charles Perkins,
    6–7
West Side Improvement Project, 19–20
whales, history of and return to New
    York City, 63–65, 65*fig*, 98
White, Jane, 35
Wild Bird Fund, 89
William C, houseboat, 14–15
Williamson, Chris, 113
Willis, Delta, 102, 113
Wohl, Adele (née Wachtel; mother), 4,
    21, 21*fig*
Wohl, Bill (brother), 12
Wohl, David (brother), 4, 7, 82
Wohl, Faith Avedon (stepmother), 12
Wohl, Howard (father), 2–5, 3*fig*, 11–12,
    21–22, 22*fig*
Wohl, Jacob and Sadie (grandparents),
    2–3
Wohl, Jennifer (sister), 12
Wohl, Lillian, (aunt), 3
Wohl, Mike (brother), 12
Woods Hole Oceanographic Institution,
    52
World War II, and the Hudson River, 9

Yamauchi, Nobuhiro "Yama," 37–38,
    37*fig*
Yonkers, 9, 53, 128*fig*, 128–30

zooplankton, 57, 60, 63, 67–68, 72, 79,
    132–34